Growing up in Boston, it was not clear to Egyptian-born
Pauline Kaldas where she fit in. As an adult, living a life
in academia while raising two daughters with her Afri-
can-American husband and returning to Egypt every 6-8
years, she works out the puzzle of her life. In response to
her experiences, Kaldas roots herself on the hyphen in
Arab-American and looks both ways.

—Frederic Hunter, *A Year at the Edge of the Jungle*.

Through ruminations and reflections on the daily nuances
of living on the hyphen, Pauline Kaldas's *Looking Both
Ways* delves into the small moments that help define and
articulate our complex twenty-first century humanity.
To the backdrop of daily life in diaspora and the major
events of the Egyptian revolution and so many subsequent
changes that have reshaped notions of home on both sides
of the Atlantic, Kaldas eschews the definitive and instead
heeds her own advice as she "settles herself on that hyphen,
looking in both directions.

—Matthew Shenoda
Tahrir Suite

Lyrical and poetic, *Looking Both Ways* takes readers on a riveting journey where Egypt and America fuse into an amalgam of patch-worked cultures and identities. From the sea to the city and through wars and revolutions, *Looking Both Ways* is a gripping memoir that inspires readers to grapple with the many meanings of home and the pains and joys of diaspora.

—Nadine Naber
Arab America: Gender, Cultural Politics, and Activism
(Associate Professor of Gender and Women's Studies at the University of Illinois, Chicago)

Looking Both Ways

Looking Both Ways

An Egyptian-American Journey

Pauline Kaldas

Looking Both Ways:
An Egyptian-American Journey
by Pauline Kaldas
© 2017 Pauline Kaldas
Cune Press, Seattle 2017
First Edition

Hardback	ISBN 9781614571971	$34.95
Paperback	ISBN 9781614571988	$19.95
eBook	ISBN 9781614572008	$9.99
Kindle	ISBN 9781614571995	$9.99

Library of Congress #: 2017002041

Cover art is from "Teta's Key" by Helen Zughaib.
www.hzuhaib.com. Used by permission.

 Aswat: Voices from a Small Planet (a new series from Cune Press)

Looking Both Ways	Pauline Kaldas
Stage Warriors	Sarah Imes Borden
Stories My Father Told Me	Helen Zughraib

 Syria Crossroads (a series from Cune Press)

The Plain of Dead Cities	Bruce McLaren
Steel & Silk	Sami Moubayed
Syria - A Decade of Lost Chances	Carsten Wieland
The Road from Damascus	Scott C. Davis
A Pen of Damascus Steel	Ali Ferzat
Leaving Syria	Bill Dienst, MD & Madi Williamson
Visit the Old City of Aleppo	Khaldoun Fansa
East of the Grand Umayyad	Sami Moubayed
White Carnations	Musa Rahum Abbas

 Bridge Between the Cultures (a series from Cune Press)

Child Labor	Thinh Nguyen
The Other Side of the Wall	Richard Hardigan
Turning Fear Into Power	Linda Sartor
Apartheid is a Crime	Mats Svensson
A Year at the Edge of the Jungle	Frederic Hunter
The Girl Ran Away	Frederic Hunter

 Cune Cune Press: www.cunepress.com | www.cunepress.info

Contents

TIME DIFFERENCE

RESOURCES

For TJ, Yasmine, and Celine

". . . to see the world with two eyes that do not always look in the same direction."

—Edwidge Danticat

Making Home

Name:
An Improvisation on Sound

FOR TWO WEEKS, I HAD NO NAME. I imagine myself a blank page, the pen poised to print. But the pen remains uncertain about which letter to curve onto the line, what configuration of loops and dots to imprint on this new body that entered unintentionally into the world. Even after nine months of expectation, my parents had not resolved the issue of my naming. In Egypt in 1961, you could leave the hospital with the name line blank and the bundle of baby in your arms. I arrived in my parents' apartment on the island of Rhoda in the middle of Cairo, still without a sound to label my existence.

The dilemma arose because of my parents' desire to follow the old fashioned method of naming in Egypt—that the child's name should begin with the same letter as the father's name—a tradition that was believed to bestow good luck on the child. Yet my parents were not traditional. My mother believed herself progressive and liberal, eager to explore the world beyond Egypt; my father had stepped away from his family's working class background to become the first to earn a college degree and was acquiring a reputation as one of the best architects in the city. Despite this, at the birth of their child, my parents retreated to an old custom—perhaps a desire to remain rooted in their culture; perhaps an awareness of how far they would ultimately move away from the traditions that ground them; perhaps an attempt to hold tight to something familiar, like grasping a banister before leaping down a flight of stairs.

My father's name begins with the letter *B*, *beh* in Arabic, the second letter of the alphabet. The choices for a female name beginning with this letter were limited. When I asked my mother about the possibilities available to them, the only one she mentioned was *Badriya*, a peasant name she told me. I've mulled this name over my tongue, enjoying the flavor of the *r* that rolls into the *y* and rises like a wave coming into shore. I'm not sufficiently steeped in the nuances of class and region to fathom the connotations attached to this name. But at times, this rejected sound attaches itself to me. My wide feet are better suited to the rural landscape of Upper Egypt where this name likely originates, and my ability to walk along the muddy banks of the Nile exceeds my prowess of stepping in heels along the concrete city streets. I can squat into sitting position to rest my body when no chairs are available, a common posture among villagers who stop at the water's edge, washing clothes and exchanging stories.

Both sides of my family originate from the rural landscape of Upper Egypt, but my mother's family's village ancestry has been fully replaced by the veneer of city sophistication. My father was the first in his family to be born in Cairo, and his birth marked his family's transition to the opportunities of urban life. He spent his youth bent over his desk studying late into the night by the dim light of a gas lamp because the house had no electricity. His exam scores admitted him to the prestigious Engineering School at Cairo University, a rare accomplishment for someone whose family had come from the countryside and who lived in one of Cairo's poorest districts. The town where my father's family originates is Abu Teeg, a small agricultural area a few miles south of Asyut. Perhaps *Badriya* is the name that holds me close to these origins. When my great-grandfather left Abu Teeg and came to Cairo to look for work, he left behind his extended family. Although I don't know them, their descendants still live in this small town, their lives continuing in a clear path.

My own life was not destined for such clarity. As my extended family entered my parent's apartment to debate the name of this new child, they must have bantered about their lives. They offered the names in their imaginations to seek out a new future for this infant—the first child to be born into the next generation of my mother's family, coming from my great-grandfather Boulos who married my great-grandmother Rifaa when she was only fourteen. Rifaa gave birth to ten children—seven brothers and one sister survived into adulthood. My mother was the first child of the one sister and the first to marry of her generation, making me the first to be born in my generation. My mother was twenty-one when I was born. Finding herself married too young and then pregnant, perhaps she felt that her dreams of travel and her desire to live in the more progressive world she saw through the fashion magazines and foreign movies would forever remain elusive. She sat with this new bundle that had arrived two weeks past the due date after a difficult labor, unable to determine a name.

The debate over my name became a family matter, and the negotiations must have tensed as names were brought forth for approval. My maternal grandfather wanted to name me *Azza*, meaning "dear one." It was a feminine version of his own name, *Aziz*, and thus an attempt to lay claim to me, his first grandchild, and, although he could not have known, the only one he would see before his unexpected death only six months after my birth. Perhaps if that had been my name, I would have been held closer to the place that birthed me, and my journey would not have taken me so far from home.

I think of the name *Azza* still tucked inside me, like a pinch of nutmeg added to heighten flavor. It is this name that pulls me back to family. My grandfather Aziz lost his parents when he was a young boy and found himself orphaned. He was taken in by his aunt and uncle who raised him along with their own two sons. He had been an only child, and when he turned eighteen, he inherited some money that his parents had left for him. He went to Paris, presumably to study art at the Sorbonne. Years later, he returned with no degree and no money; the stories that circulated said he had spent his money on women and alcohol. Aziz was social and charming, and I suspect he must have acquired numerous friends who were attracted to him either by his charisma or his generous spirit. I imagine this man, known for his artistic ability, his elaborate handwriting, and his tendency toward extravagance. My own handwriting is plain and solid, following the pattern of my engineer father, and my drawings remain flat. When my grandfather returned to Egypt, he became, like so many others, a government civil servant. He married my grandmother who must have strained her anger each time he squandered money as she tried to stretch his small salary far enough to raise her children and to present a respectable household.

It was my aunt Vicky who ultimately offered a word that appeased the needs of tradition and modernity. "Pauline," she said. Like so many of that time, Aunt Vicky was French educated, and her fluency in the language must have given her an elevated status. This name, with its foreign pronunciation, its removal from the Arabic language—still perceived as inferior in this post-colonial society—must have caught my mother's ear. Coming from another language, it allowed a glimpse into a world outside the confines of Nasser's socialist regime with its insistence on isolation. It opened the possibility of so much that was forbidden at the time, the limitations on imports turning things like nuts and chocolates into taboo delicacies. Yet the name still followed the tradition of repetition. Since the letter *P* did not exist in the Arabic language, it would begin with *beh*, the same letter that began my father's name.

It was with this christening of name that, unknown to the family gathered together in those days, my destiny as a bridge between these two languages and all they carried began. This name marked my place at the periphery of the world I was born into and which became mine.

"Pauline" in 1961 Egypt was a combination of sounds that required too much effort in shaping the mouth and manipulating the tongue. I became a chameleon at a young age, adapting to the call of my names. Most of my family called me *Paula* but pronounced it *Bola*, since the soft *P* existed neither in sound nor form in Arabic. This pronunciation was a bilingual combination of sound to adapt my European name to the post-colonial world of Egypt, a rounded abbreviation of the elongated name that molded itself into the Arabic language and created something that rolled easily from the tongue.

One uncle, wanting to be proper, tried to use my full name, but his pronunciation could not touch the softness of that English *P*, and his spelling could only present a direct transliteration, recreating me as *Boleen*. The letters tumbled over each other, crammed into this singular sound. My uncle had manifested this English name onto the rules of the Arabic language where there are no silent letters. The precise translation of sounds used to write my name in Arabic—*beh, wow, lam, yeh, noon*—placed emphasis on the first syllables rather than the second, thus creating a new articulation of this name. At the British school I attended, I expect that my teachers pronounced my name correctly and perhaps acquired an additional fondness for this small Egyptian student who arrived with the English language already imprinted on her. The variations of spellings and pronunciations must have frustrated my mother who had studied English Literature in college. She had selected the name, catching it like a rope to swing across the ocean, so she could latch onto another shore. Perhaps it was my name that gave her the courage to initiate our emigration.

I lost many things when we immigrated, among them the alternate pronunciations and spellings of my name as well as one middle name. Names in Egypt are the line of genealogy connecting us back to our ancestors, so our names are infinite. The child's first name is followed by the first name of the father, grandfather, great-grandfather, etc. A child might go back two generations when giving their name; as they get older, they are more likely to stop at their father's name. These names are an assertion of identity and history, so when I say my name is Pauline Bahig Anwar Kaldas, I place myself in the world as *Pauline*, the daughter of *Bahig*, who is the son of *Anwar*, who is the son of *Kaldas*. Genealogy becomes deeply imbedded into the language by which we name ourselves. There is no discussion of middle names when a child is born, nothing about what will sound good with the first name or the expectation that a girl will have a female middle name; all middle names are male since it's the paternal line that is passed down from one generation to the next. I expect this can be traced back to the laws of inheritance and men being the ones who acquire money and pass it on to their offspring. That lineage is vital, so women in Egypt don't change their names when they marry. We are born with our identities already intact, and they remain permanent.

When my father filled out the paperwork for our emigration, he was told that America allows only one middle name and that all of us had to have the same last name. Confronted with this dilemma, and being a practical man, my father made the necessary adjustments. For his name, he kept his father's name as the middle name and used his grandfather's name as his last name. For my mother, he kept her father's name as her middle name but changed her last name to his side of the family. And for me, he kept his name as my middle name and dropped my grandfather's name, so my great-grandfather's name could be used as my last name. Thus, all the names that had existed continued in some configuration. He held his father's name and I held his name. It was a method of safekeeping, reflecting my father's desire to save everything that might be necessary in the future.

There was also the matter of spelling our last name. I've been told that my great-grandfather's given name might have been *Kaladios*, an old Coptic name, but, like so many names, it is simplified and shortened when spoken, becoming *Kaldas*—its long ending dropped and its pronunciation changed. With the transition from classical to colloquial Arabic, the hard *K* sound marked by the letter *qaf* in Arabic is changed to the *A* sound, a common transformation in the spoken language. When my father wrote it on the forms, he kept the shorter version but attempted the correct classical Arabic spelling, with *K* being the closest sound to the original *qaf*—a somersault transformation of letters that reverberate with the past as sound moves across oceans and plants itself into a new setting.

When I returned to Egypt as an adult, one of my cousins declared that I needed a nickname, an appropriately Egyptian one, and she dubbed me *Lina*. I was grateful for the alternative, a name I didn't have to repeat when I left it with my clothes at the drycleaner or with my order at the grocery store. I used it often, reasserting myself into a homeland from which I had been separated even at my birth by my given name.

Naming my own children proved to be even more complex and required a longer process. The first names came easily, and my husband and I had decided they would have his last name. It was the middle names that made me stumble. In the end, I retrieved my loss and exacted my revenge against the American rules of naming that my father was required to follow. I bestowed two middle names on each child, creating chaos on the lines of applications that demand the consistency of one middle name.

Initially, I gave my oldest daughter, Yasmine, my grandmother's first name, *Aida*, as a middle name, in some ways following the American tradition by giving her a feminine name and one that connected her to another woman in the family. When my younger daughter, Celine, was born, I feared the loss of my own last name through the generations and gave her *Kaldas* as a middle name, following neither the American tradition of bestowing a daughter with a female middle name nor the Arab tradition of putting in the first name of the father.

Around the time Yasmine was eight, she came home from school to announce that another child had told her we could not all be one family because we didn't have the same last name. It had never occurred to me to change my last name when I married. At my daughter's announcement, smoke practically circled out of my ears, anger at anyone denying our unity as a family. But something more was triggered. I struggled until I made my way to the court house and added a middle name for each of my children.

I put *Kaldas* in the middle of Yasmine's name, thus asserting the family lineage into her identity. For Celine, I added *Aziza*, another feminine variation of *Aziz*, finally fulfilling my grandfather's request that a child would be named after him. After the official designation of these additions and all the paperwork that finally yielded new birth certificates, I sensed a slight shifting in my children. My older daughter's gentle nature acquired a new layer of determination (some would call it stubbornness or hard headedness), a clear mark of everyone in the Kaldas family. It was also at this moment that my younger daughter's artistic inclinations began to emerge, as if Aziz's artistic ability had found a new place to settle. She made her way through reams of papers, beginning her pictures of little girls by drawing their small feet and then making her way up until a hand holding a balloon appeared on the page, like an image that believes in its own existence.

My daughters muddle with these names, unsure of which middle name to put down when there is only space for one, and the records through their young lives, from medical forms to school report cards, display an assortment of identities. The first and last name anchors them, but in between, identity shifts and sways through generations of people moving over land and water to create new lives.

I think of my children returning from kindergarten, showing me how they played the name game where each child creates a gesture of movement by which to identify themselves, an utterance of body that exists outside of spoken language. Its simplicity articulated by a child appears to hold more truth than all the linguistic configurations by which we have chosen to name our existence in the world.

Nostalgia for Home

I HAVE TRIED TO FIND MY CHILDHOOD HOME several times, asking the taxi driver to zigzag his way through the tight streets of Mohandessein, while I attempt to recollect my Uncle Fouad's directions along with my Aunt Alice's memory of the location. They're not identical—Uncle Fouad says we lived on Riyad Street and Aunt Alice says it was a side street off of Riyad.

While visiting my family in Egypt, I tried once again to get my older relatives to recall the exact location. But it was my cousin Ashraf who spoke up and claimed he knew the precise address. Ashraf is a year or two younger than me, which means he might have been seven in 1969 when my parents and I left Egypt and immigrated to the United States. How could he carry this memory of place for so many years? When I returned to Egypt after twenty-two years and met him again, I recognized him by the rhythm of his voice, a soothing harmony that retrieved my childhood. He and his sister, Mona, visited us often, and the three of us spent afternoons in games of hide and seek and evenings playing Monopoly together. Ashraf and Mona served as my brother and sister, eliminating the loneliness that came from being an only child.

Ashraf agreed to take me to my childhood home, and we drove from my aunt's house in Giza to the neighboring town of Mohandessein. In the 1960s, Mohandessein was a new neighborhood, attracting those families attempting to rise above the middle class. Its streets were wide, and the villas only two stories with large gardens framing them. Now, like the rest of Cairo, it had become congested, the roads narrowing with too many buildings and cars parked along the sidewalks. Ashraf maneuvered the streets with an instinctive memory. The sun hovered at a standstill, just before it would begin to set.

We made a turn, and Ashraf pulled the car to a stop. When we stepped out, he pointed across the street to a house. The front entrance and the upstairs balcony tugged beneath my skin, like an old photograph slipping out of an abandoned book. This two-story beige stucco house had remained while my life had been transported to another place. But the terrace that extended on the side of our first floor villa apartment where I spent my summer days playing jump rope and skip ball was gone. I knew it would be. Land became too precious as the population grew, and removing that terrace made room for another apartment building that could become home to new tenants and provide income for another landlord.

A young security guard with a rifle strapped over his shoulder stood by the front door, an indication that whoever lived there now was some kind of dignitary. I wasn't surprised—my aunts and uncles still talk about the beauty of that villa apartment with its three spacious bedrooms, the formal salon with its green tapestried furniture for entertaining guests, and the massive dining room with its shining oval table to host elaborate events. Now, with so many of these two-story villas turned into high rises, the memory of this home continues to spark the imagination and desires of my family.

The guard's presence meant we had to keep our distance, so we stayed across the street as I snapped a few pictures of the house. By the time the guard started walking toward us, we were driving away. But I knew what was behind the front door: the way you immediately found yourself in the living room—the couch where I sat learning how to work needlepoint by imitating the cross-stitches my mother taught me, the room where I slept on the small bed covered in a silky green fabric while listening to my father drawing at his architect's table, the large bathroom with the black and white tiles where I squatted next to the washer woman in front of the tub full of soapy water as she scrubbed each article of clothing with the balls of her palms. The rest of the apartment is a map imprinted on my body, each room a silhouette I've framed and can still enter.

What I couldn't see was the garden behind the house, and I wondered if it had encountered the same fate as the terrace, taken over by another apartment building. Maybe it was better not to know. My memory paints it as a landscape of abundance and hidden sanctuaries. I wandered its paths, stumbling upon new discoveries—the grape arbor, the guava tree, the sweet lemon tree, the mango tree. But I'm suspicious of my memory—Was the garden really so large? Were there really so many trees? Still I'm reluctant to give up my exaggerated nostalgia.

This is my first home, but my mother remembers an earlier one, where my memory can't reach. It's the first apartment she and my father shared on the island of Rhoda in the middle of the Nile, and it is where I was born. The island is small, stretching from Garden City to Old Cairo. Originally filled with lush gardens, creating an oasis of fruit and flowering trees, it still holds the mystery of the past. According to Arab tradition, Moses was placed on the banks of this island by his mother and later found by the Pharaoh's daughter.

Over time, the island has become another residential area in the overcrowded city. My parents lived on this island for perhaps two years. When I was only six months old, my grandfather died, and my parents eventually had to find a larger place so my grandmother and my aunt could move in with us. My father rented the apartment in Mohandessein. Its name literally means "the engineers," and it enticed new residents by offering cheaper prices to those in the engineering profession. We settled our lives in this new location, while my father worked three jobs to support all of us.

My childhood was punctuated by a recurring nightmare of robbers breaking into our house and chasing me from room to room—when they find me and catch me, pressing their hands into my back, I wake up screaming. I never knew where the dream came from until I learned that after my grandfather's death, someone broke into my grandmother's apartment, stealing her jewelry. My grandmother grew afraid of living alone with her younger daughter, so my parents moved into a larger apartment that had room for all of us. The story I heard must have seeped into my child's mind and transformed itself into the terror that entered my dreams.

The apartment in Rhoda is my mother's nostalgia for home, the first two years of her young marriage. There was some happiness in that small apartment and my parents' attempt to set up home as a new couple. That was before the move to Mohandessein with the arrival of extended family. I was oblivious—only happy to have more adults who could pay attention to me. We lived in Mohandessein for eight years. When we emigrated, my grandmother and aunt moved in with an older uncle, and we sold the furniture, leaving the apartment with empty rooms.

***

For an immigrant, home moves from experience to memory quickly, like the sharp push on a swing. I carry my first memory of home with me, tucked inside my pocket like the blue stone meant to bring good luck and keep evil away. It's hidden in the folds of my clothing, a shield to protect from what might hurt. I am a one-and-a-half generation immigrant, leaving at the age of eight and arriving in America with the clarity of my first family, food, home, streets, and language still vivid. With the turn of immigration, these experiences embedded themselves inside me, and I kept them, making their survival infinite. For an immigrant, home moves from experience to memory quickly, like the sharp push on a swing.

But home also precedes memory, a folded page in the mind. Both my parents carried loss of home even before their immigration. They grew up in the midst of Nasser's regime with its promise of social mobility for those who had found their opportunities soldered shut by colonial hierarchy. My mother remembers sitting on the balcony of her grandfather's house situated on the Nile in the town of Maadi. She stretched her vision across the water to see further than land and nation. When Nasser became president, his regime took away from the wealthy, claiming to distribute among the masses, and the house was lost. Instead, my mother grew up in the lap of a middle class family, straining their means to make an appearance of upper class sophistication.

My father was the first one born in Cairo, marking his family's migration from the village of Abu Teeg in Upper Egypt to the greater opportunities in the city of Cairo. Family, home, and land were left behind to build a new future. Instead of the village, my father grew up in the house my great-grand-father built in Old Cairo with its small rooms and no electricity. Each night, he returned home from long days of school and jobs to study by the light of a gas lamp, squinting his eyes against the intruding darkness.

Home is passed on through my parents' memories—it is my mother's recollection of family gatherings at the eldest uncle's house, the first born of my great-grandmother Rifaa and my great-grandfather Boulos. This uncle gathered his six brothers and one sister with their offspring at his apartment in Maadi. Our family was whole then, a few kilometers between each home, an easy ride to reach one another. My mother remembers these gatherings as impromptu, a thread of whispers to guide them all to this place at the same time. I must have been there too, among so many before the possibility of a new world tugged at everyone's imagination. But when I see us gathering in laughter—the adults towering above me, the platters of stuffed grape leaves and cabbage leaves plucked by everyone's fingers, someone offering me a morsel of grilled lamb like a communion of bread—I can't be sure whether it's my own or my mother's remembrance that has placed this memory inside me.

My mother transplanted her memories when she immigrated. We cele-brated Christmas and Easter at our house in Boston—a circle of people gathering around the tight kitchen counter, my mother holding court as she orchestrates the dinner. Voices modulate in the comfort of Arabic broken by the higher pitch of English, still accented by those who immigrated even forty years ago, disrupted by the practiced tones of my second-generation cousins whose English flows like a stream until an Arabic word falls from their mouths like a pebble. My own voice weighs itself on a swinging bridge—my learned

English is fluent until I hear my relatives' English, and then it retreats into the first years of my broken mouth where only garbled sounds reached my ears and I could not utter this new language. This gathering inside my parent's home was bought with the hard labor of those early years, proving themselves again in this new land.

Aunt Helena

There are not millions of deaths. It happens millions of times that someone dies.
— Etel Adnan, *Sitt Marie Rose*

A WEEK AFTER I TURNED SIX, THE WAR BEGAN. We must have celebrated my birthday with the usual family gathering—as an only child and the first of my generation to be born, my birthdays were an occasion to celebrate with aunts, uncles, and grandparents, pulling together our large extended family. I know we went to Groppi's pastry shop to pick out my cake, and I'm sure I selected the most elaborate one with chocolate swirls rising and twisting into a sculpture of confection. A few days later, I might have sensed the pattern of energy changing, the suppressed tones of urgency, the hesitant movements, or perhaps there was nothing but our daily lives until the surprise of that first day when heightened fear entered each house.

What I remember is the way dusk brought the town crier to our street, swinging a lantern and commanding us to turn off our lights. He seemed a comical figure, this man waving a lamp down the street. I peered out the window to catch a glimpse of him, but I know that hands tugged me back inside as footsteps moved more rapidly, and my grandmother's arms gathered us into a circle to sit on the floor in the living room, one stubby candle placed in the middle. The excitement of an event seeped in—we were all there, even my father who was usually away working several jobs, my mother who was often out with friends, my aunt who was still in college, and my grandmother. We held hands, linking ourselves together. Once the droning of airplane engines above us began, someone blew out the candle, and we sat still and silent in pitch black with only our sense of hearing to guide us. When I asked questions, I was shushed with half-whispered answers. The planes above us droned loudly, a heavy monotone of sound breaking through air. As long as we stayed in this deep darkness, they could not see us. And we could not become a target for the bombs they carried. The entire city blanketed itself in the cover of night like a magic trick, so pilots believed they were flying over empty land. For six nights, we repeated our pattern. Fear settled inside me, heightened by what my mind imagined—the loss of any of us, the extinction of our existence. I sat still, listening for pauses in the humming air above us.

When the candle burned down and the air lifted giving way to clear sky, we emerged to find ourselves shattered by loss.

At family gatherings, I watched my Aunt Helena, my great grandmother's sister. She sat upright in a chair, her hands folded on her lap, her heavy body without motion like a model posing for an artist's canvas. A statue carved to imitate life. Her eyes stared into the distance to a place beyond the room where we sat, beyond the walls that framed us. Sadness filled her face and she spoke to no one, her lips sealed into a silence that followed her gaze. I tugged at someone's sleeve to ask why she looked like that, and I understood that her son had not returned from the war, that his body could not be found, that she mourned in that space between loss and hope. My Aunt Helena had entered a place from which she could never return. Only her body remained with us as she looked beyond where she sat to see her son, will him home from wherever he had gone missing. Her body carried that loss to her own death.

Her son, my Uncle Wadi, whose name means calm and peaceful, was a doctor who had been called to enter the war like so many young men. My memory recalls only a vague blur of his existence, a brush stroke that suggests a man who carried himself with kindness. I remember him lifting me off the ground for a hug, a gentleness to his embrace. Every family in Egypt lost someone in the war, the losses tearing gaps like open wounds. My uncle's absence became an empty space among his three siblings: my Aunt Alice, my Aunt Vicky, and my Uncle Makram. Two sisters and a brother who inherited their mother's loss. They still speak of him—Wadi, who was lost in the war, whose body was never found, whose mother could never finish mourning, whose success as a doctor was lost. His place in the family remains open as if one day he could still return.

They suspect he was killed by a mine, perhaps in the Sinai desert, his body shattered by the explosion. Aunt Helena continued to hold onto that translucent thread of hope that one day her son might return. Each of his siblings has lived well into their eighties, as if he bequeathed his lost years to them. Israel won the six day war of June 1967, and Egypt's defeat poured into each home, a devastated country losing the Sinai Peninsula, losing the battle to regain the Palestinian homeland, and losing its power as a nation. My parents, like so many others after the war, lost faith in their homeland and looked elsewhere, becoming part of the brain drain that pulled many in

Egypt to emigrate and begin new lives in another world. For me, the war of 1967 is marked by the sadness of my Aunt Helena's face, her still body, and her distant gaze, when I understood how far loss can take you, that the living can follow the dead and never return.

Mediterranean Waves

I GREW UP INSIDE MEDITERRANEAN WAVES, each summer the sea beckoning like an old friend. We travelled to Alexandria for a month and spent our days between sand and water. I remember plastic shovels, a red bucket, the tools of sand castles built inside fortresses circled by a moat.

My father taught me to swim on my back, his hands beneath me to align my body against the surface. I struggled to keep my head back, to trust the buoyancy of salt water. Cautiousness made me lift my head, and my body caved into the sea until I caught my balance and again found breath.

My mother entered the water with trepidation, hand held tight to my father's. The lapping of sea at the sand's edge tickling her ankles made her tighten her grip and hesitate her steps. As each wave receded, she edged forward, wary of the next one's approach. The sea's calling enticed her only to her waist, until a wave reached higher to caress her face; then she would dash back to safety.

The waves leaped against us. We bounced to avoid their impact, but sprinklings of salt still slapped our taste buds.

Those summers, I learned the freedom of the sea's expanse. In the distance, a boat's silhouette traced the edge of the water's horizon until it faded into a place beyond my imagination. My small life between school and home in Cairo and the sea in Alexandria were enough to satisfy my desires.

But like the refrain of waves, forces push against my world, and the tug of childhood begins to release. In 1969, the war remains a layer beneath our lives. I see it in my great aunt's eyes that look beyond to a place where she imagines her son still alive. I sense it in the diminished ambitions that fray at the tapestry of my parents' generation. Their gaze longs for a new landscape, roads paved in metallic hope.

America is a word void of images. Here coarse sand trickles between my toes, salt stings my tongue, fish snatch at my nostrils, rising voices blend in my ears, and waves tapping against shore capture my sight.

And I find myself again, as one photograph holds me. I am just five, maybe six. My body turns to the camera, eyes slightly lowered to shield from the sun's strength, arm bent and hand on my hip in a gesture almost aggressive against the camera. In my other hand, I hold the red bucket with a picture of a sailboat. My hair frames around my face with short curly bangs that hover above my eyes. Standing in my two-piece bathing suit, I curl my toes into the slippery water and my body pushes forward in a gesture of defiance against this intrusion. This is all I had to carry across the ocean with me—the sand of my homeland and the defiance held in that pose, that hand placed on my waist in daring. But in this moment, I am as yet unaware of how the sea will beckon me to cross beyond the horizon's edge and reach a world that stretches beyond my vision.

I am held in the trance of this world that circles desert and sea. My feet slap tight in hard leather against the concrete streets of Cairo, and my arches sway over the sand shifting on these Alexandria beaches. I am eight before we leave and I have learned to carry my weight across these terrains.

A Dictionary, a Bible
&
a Romance Novel

RECLINED INTO THE CORNER of the light blue velvet couch in the living room, I'm hunting for a word in our large red dictionary. Today's word begins with *f* and ends with a hard *k* sound. My parents are still at work, and I can take my time browsing through the dictionary, deciphering the meanings of the hard monosyllabic sounds being bantered about in the school playground. These are new words, uttered by classmates whose brash loudness remains an enigma to my upbringing of proper and respectful behavior. I flip the pages, distracted by other words, captured by the possibility of meaning.

This is my daily routine each day after coming home from fifth grade. I carry these new words inside my mouth, so I can look them up when I get home. The red dictionary was one of my parents' first purchases after arriving. It sits next to the small green Arabic/English dictionary that travelled across the ocean tucked into our suitcases. I spent the first year flipping the thin flimsy paper, but I couldn't decipher the path from Arabic to English—too much slipped between the pages. These curved and twisted letters, decorated by dots, offered little guidance into the world of mumbled nasal sounds where meaning tucked itself beneath bland expressions and un-gestured hands.

I find the word and read the definition. The meaning eludes me, but the ugliness of its intention is clear. I understand enough to put this word among others I have heard—words thrown like water balloons that sometimes break into explosions and sometimes fall flat against the ground. I place these words in a pouch, pull the strings to shut them in. At some point they might prove their usefulness, but for now I'm only a listener.

It's later when I'm a teenager trapped on the high wire between cultures that I begin to mumble these words under my breath. In retaliation against my parents' restrictions and their disapproval of my Americanized behavior, I swing these words, but never aloud. The hard consonants appease my desire for assertion. Later, as an adult, my frustration will find satisfaction in the sharp expressions of Arabic. Even in translation, my husband and daughters can't grasp their full meaning. The desire to express anger without being understood keeps me well-versed in the swear words of both languages. When my younger daughter bounces her first illicit word at home, she looks in expectant horror at me, anticipating my reprimand. I shrug—anger and frustration require expression, and these are the words we use as we grow. Once, at the age of three, angry at her father and not yet having learned these sharp words, she turned against him and said, "A plague of popsicles upon your house," her small voice releasing the heaviness of emotion.

As a child, I learn that not all words carry the same weight; some are daffodils bending in the breeze, some are tree branches swaying in wind, and some are rough edged rocks deliberately thrown. Measuring with the delicacy of an old scale, I teach myself how to balance my words across the page.

***

My nighttime readings are the stories from an English language children's Bible. I read them to return to the small bed where my grandmother sat while I was being tucked into sleep. My request for a story yielded one of these Biblical tales told from my grandmother's memory, her voice giving rise to each story's moral conflict, holding my attention as I learned to anticipate that narrative arc, waiting for the climax of Joseph's brothers discovering his true identity, of God taking back his command for Abraham to kill Isaac, of Noah building the ark in time to escape the flood. I held onto the edge of her words, waiting for resolution.

In English, this book only approximates the flavor of my grandmother's lost voice. The color illustrations replace the sound of these stories as I fall asleep each night. I pull at the threads of my memory to call up the imaginations of my mind when I listened to her.

These are my first stories, and I carry them in my grandmother's voice, the rhythm and beat of language teaching me how to translate from one world to another.

***

I'm a latchkey child, although there is no name for it in the early 1970s. I return home from school every day, pull the string that holds the key around my neck, unlock the front door, and enter into the quiet walls of our house. My boredom leads me to snooping. I climb up kitchen counters to rummage through the dark corners of cabinets, hoping to find something sweet to appease my craving. I browse through the drawers, rarely finding anything of interest until one day in the bottom of my mother's dresser, I discover a book. It's thick and the cover displays a woman with flowing dark hair, the sleeve of her dress falling off her shoulder and her face suspended in a perpetual look of bewildered surprise. This is an unexpected find since I've only seen my mother flipping the pages of housekeeping magazines, searching out home decorating ideas and new recipes for dinner parties. I settle myself cross-legged in front of the open dresser drawer and within view of the window where I can see the bus that drops my mother off after work.

I begin to read, immediately captured by the sultry language that lights my young imagination. When my eye catches the bus rolling down our street, I memorize the page I'm on and replace the book back into the drawer, carefully folded into the clothing. Each day after school, I repeat my performance, making my way through this adventure of a woman captured by pirates, the captain's charm too enticing to resist. This saga of sexual seduction is a foray into the world of desire that I'm just beginning to understand. Without being told, I know these are not topics to be broached in my home. I give only a fleeting thought to the meaning of my mother reading this book. It takes weeks to make my way through this novel; each day there is only so much time before the bus returns my mother home, and on weekends I have to restrain myself.

I learn the temptation of words, the way they entice us into a world outside our own, the way each story stretches us out of our own living room of existence. This pirate ship with its heroine traversing the seas shows me that words can take you to places of wild wanderings. It is the body unraveled and taken out of confinement.

***

These were the three English books in our house: the dictionary, the children's Bible, and my mother's romance novel. They framed a window through which I could seek out a pathway to open language, to replenish my words, to speak with this intractable voice.

Catching Windows

RIDING IN THE BACK SEAT OF MY PARENTS' CAR—moving through darkened city streets—the humming of wheels on asphalt—this lullaby of evening traffic—the silence of our voices—if we don't speak then the monotone of our speed through air remains unbroken—I stretch my eyes into the terrain outside—an angle of light illuminates vision—pin my sight to the window of a house or apartment—a glimpse of a room: a vase, a table, a bookcase, the corner of a bed—creating a composition from still life—sometimes a shadow of figure fleeting—imagining other lives—a couple eating take-out Chinese food, a woman leaning over open books, a child playing with blocks—so many ways to live in the world—my flights of fantasy bordering this rectangle of space—

encapsulated in this interior—tight embrace of our three-person family—my intense curiosity about how others live—what they eat—how they arrange their furniture—in what tone they speak to one another—my mother dreamt me on the other side of the ocean and could not reach me— just a dream I say—but I'm already travelling across water—penetrating this American life—peering into windows—to place myself reading next to a dim lamp or in a kitchen stirring a pot—anyone but the only child of immigrants overtly conscious of the difference of my life—looking through glass to catch some glimpse of the norm of living—do others sit down to meals of stuffed zucchini or fava beans—do their parents' arguments circle around to the past and before the past to relatives in another country where the sun sets seven hours earlier—I'm digging through tunnels to reach these windows—imagining myself into an American life of simple foods and a freedom into un-prescribed relationships—the possibility of creating myself in another frame—

another car and another memory in Egypt—maybe 6/7/8 years old— when does memory begin?—my father driving—my mother next to him— in the back I sit behind my father—next to me the young servant girl who works for us—maybe just a year or two older—I think of her as my equal—

can't differentiate the hierarchy of the adult world—she is the only one close
to my age and she likes to play—I want to take her with us on our summer
vacation to Alexandria and cry when my parents say no—the car skimming
these Cairo streets—for a moment we are stranded—the illusion of a family
of four—

in America in the backseat—trapped in a box of Egyptian culture packed
and shipped at the end of 1969—that box sat in each place we inhabited—
the first apartment on Appleton Street with my aunt and uncle—the second
on Fenno Street by ourselves—the first house where my father put all his
savings as down payment—and the second house renovated twice to stylize
the American dream—that box tied me in knots—no slumber parties, no
boyfriends, no apartment—a gridlock of a transplanted culture in stasis—so
I looked into the windows of houses and apartments as we drove the streets
of Boston—to draw the outline of my shadow into another life—each
reflection offering a possibility of deviation—I could be a student, studying
for an exam; I could be living with my boyfriend, sharing a simple meal
of noodles; I could be hosting a party, mingling with friends—my eyes
stretched their imagination—placing me in each scene—released from the
tight air of the car—until I am framed inside each window—

tight triangle of three—an only child enters beyond the periphery of
emotion—centered as the target of anger and love in simultaneous doses—
rowing across an ocean to escape—held inside the airtight grip of a car—
imagining these lives unfettered by expectations—not the status of marriage
and family but the open space of living alone pulls me toward these lighted
frames—to exist—unmoored from family—

what happens to us when we trim ourselves off and travel across oceans—
the weave of family that kept us in its grasp reluctantly releases—and this
nucleus exists in isolation—I dream of houses with rooms inside rooms—an
architectural maze that opens and closes in unexpected configurations—a
three-dimensional jigsaw puzzle—sometimes in a dream, I stumble into a
new room in my own home—an accidental opening—and I wake—certain
I could step into a discovery of new space—

my dream's eye stretches—an angle of light holds a panel of glass—
caught off guard by a moving life I can barely detect—a small frame

opening—fabricated by American dreams—each generation taking flight—landing onto an unchartered path— even now when the car edges toward my own home, I look up—wonder at the life inside these windows as if it were not my own—only an act of imagination—

Upsizing

M Y PARENTS ARE RENOVATING THEIR HOUSE AGAIN. My mother explains that the paint on the outside is peeling, and the wood has to be replaced. She's right. During our visits over the past several years, we've noticed the deterioration of the exterior. But it has taken my mother a while to decide what she wants. My father has been waiting patiently. After all these years, he knows not to force her into making a decision or influence her; otherwise, he will bear the brunt of her disappointment. This is inevitable. As inevitable as the fact that my mother will not settle for simply fixing the outside. Her goal is to transform the house from a 1970s contemporary design —an architectural style that no longer pleases her despite her original infatuation with it— to a modern traditional home. As the plans fall into place with her decision to replace the exterior with cedar wood and add several gables, she decides that since the front of the house is being changed, she will also widen the foyer.

The small space where people gather as they enter and leave gets crowded with guests, especially given the length of Egyptian goodbyes. The end of each visit is marked by kisses on both cheeks, questions about the well-being of each member of the family, and plans for the next time we will get together, as well as thanks for the meal that was eaten and an exchange of recipes. This process is lengthy. My husband, who comes from a solid American family that says goodbye with a quick hug and a thank you, has now learned that when someone in my family announces that it's time to go, he can anticipate an additional hour or two before the actual departure takes place. To accommodate this ritual, the foyer will become expansive, allowing for an even longer ceremony of greetings and goodbyes. This of course will require a new front door and a custom-made window above the door.

The new foyer will also contain additional storage space because my father has never discarded a single letter, bank statement, receipt, or any piece of paper—all of which are tightly packed in boxes with no labels to identify them. These boxes have been piled in step-pyramid fashion in the closet of the upstairs study. This arrangement could have been acceptable except for the fact that my mother resents the intrusion of these boxes because it allows less space for her clothing. Apparently, there is little consolation in having four other closets that serve as the recipients of her wardrobe. It is the principle of the thing, she explains, asserting that my father should not be saving these unnecessary papers and that they are the cause of the clutter in their home. Thus, two closets will be added to the design of the foyer; these are placed at a higher level, requiring a full-length ladder to reach them. And this is where my father's collection of boxes will reside.

Since the foyer will be expanded and the half bath is right off the foyer, my parents will now push out the front of the house in order to create space for a full bath. This, my mother claims, is completely my father's fault. Ever since his brother had to be in a wheelchair, my father has asserted the need for a full bath on the main floor in fear that either of them might end up in the same position. On a rare night when I happen to call and my mother is out, my father, who is a plumbing engineer, assures me that there is no actual need for a full bath. You can simply secure a shower head in the ceiling and make that work in extenuating circumstances. However, my mother is adamant that a full bath has to be added to appease my father. This bathroom will include an original tile design with a wave of blue glass across the wall as well as an Italian vanity and a custom-fitted shower system—there is no doubt that it will be worthy of a fold-out section in *Architectural Digest*.

With this new addition, the washer and dryer will now be moved from the kitchen to the bathroom, providing additional storage space for the pots and pans, the serving platters, and the Showtime Rotisserie bought through the TV infomercial. Naturally, this will lead to the space of the old bathroom being added to the family room, which also needs to have the floor-to-ceiling glass window replaced since it has been leaking, and if they are going to replace the window, then they're going to extend the family room, which, my mother explains, has always been too small when she invites people over, so now there will be enough space for the multitude of guests, allowing them to fill the room comfortably and spill over into the octagonal sun room that was added with the last renovation. When I mention the more formal living room and dining room that are rarely used, she continues describing how the window in the family room will now become a door which will require the addition of a deck because you can't have a door that goes out to nothing and that means they might as well expand the rest of the deck and have it wrap around the back of the house to overlook the backyard that will fall into shambles as a result of the construction—but new landscaping will come later—and in that case one of the windows in the living room—that I have already mentioned is never used—will also be turned into a door that can go out onto the deck. I decide it's time to end our phone conversation when all of this begins to make sense.

***

My parents are both in their seventies. According to our understanding of the stages of life, they should be downsizing. Clearly, they seem to have over-looked this. Their desire for expansion and the constant renewing of their home appears essential to the core of their being. Perhaps my parents' down-sizing stage has already taken place. When we emigrated from Egypt in 1969, the three of us arrived with the six suitcases that were permitted on interna-tional flights, their contents carefully selected from our three bedroom villa apartment. Our home had been meticulously furnished when my parents married, each room's decor carefully negotiated between my mother and grandmother: the ornate dark mahogany bedroom set my grandmother chose, the grand contemporary oval dining room table my mother craved, the tapestried furniture for the formal salon that served as an enticement into the world of British royalty. Every item was sold for less than its value, including my grandmother's piano with her name engraved on it, her claim as the original owner permanently marked in its wooden frame.

From what remained, my parents packed those six suitcases. They had to decide what to take and what to release permanently. My mother was thirty and my father was thirty-six, an entire lifetime already lived. They distilled the accumulations of their life into six suitcases, carried across continents and oceans to sustain them in the new world they were about to enter. Little of those contents remain now.

Except, a few years ago, my mother opened one of her five closets and offered me my grandmother's dress. It's a long silky red dress, the silhouette design patterned with circles of gold. It was sewn by my grandmother, and her stitches are still tight and intimate, holding two roses at the neckline with pearls tucked in their center. The dress exemplifies another place and time. It was worn by a different woman than the grandmother I remember, her sadness heavy in her body after my grandfather's unexpected heart attack. What made my grandmother relinquish this single dress, agree to have it travel across time, and, with so little space, what made my mother ask if she could have it, knowing there would likely be no place in the new world to wear such a dress?

Also, not long ago, I was filling out an application that required the date

I was granted citizenship, and I had to ask my father for the information. I watched him dig through his boxes, searching for that one letter that marked my permanent acceptance into this new country. He pulled out cardboard tubes, explaining that inside them were drawings of the projects he had done as a young architect in Egypt. By the time we emigrated, he had already acquired a solid reputation in his field. The last time we were in Egypt, as we drove through the streets of Cairo, my uncle pointed out the buildings my father had helped to design, his signature still left on the city skyline. These tubes must have claimed a precious place in those suitcases.

There is another item that also found a place on our journey. It is tucked somewhere deep in the storage of my parents' home—a box of photos from our first life. Pictures of my parents' wedding, their heads crowned and bent toward the priest blessing them, a picture of me holding a pail and shovel at the edge of the Mediterranean, the three of us sitting in front of the piano the night before we left. These photos tumble with no albums to hold them, memories that still float unexpectedly into our new lives.

The rest of the luggage must have been filled with carefully selected articles of clothing and shoes, items now long gone, inadequate for the new terrain of America. Perhaps this kind of downsizing can only be done once. The rest of my parents' lives have been spent retrieving and replacing what could not fit in those suitcases, and their home with its constant renovations and transformation is a new life expanded and recreated to contain everything they now carry.

In Transit

Shango: A Biography

O N OUR WAY TO DO SOME ERRANDS with little time to spare, my boyfriend, TJ, suddenly swerved into the parking lot of the pet store. "Why are we here?" I asked. "I just want to stop for a minute," he insisted. He was fascinated by that small pet store, and I tried to be patient despite our limited time as we wandered the aisles, looking at fish, turtles, and insects that I couldn't imagine anyone wanting for a pet. This time, I lost track of where he was until I heard his voice, "Pauline, come here." I sensed his urgent tone and found my way to where he was in one corner of the store. He was standing outside the enclosed area where they kept the reptiles. But he wasn't looking at a snake or lizard. He was talking to a small gray striped kitten sitting in a cage. At least that is what he claimed as he spoke and the kitten responded to him with a clear meow.

This was not a pet store that carried cats and dogs, so this kitten sitting in a small cage among the reptiles was a rare sight. It turned out that someone who worked in the store had a friend whose cat had had kittens. This one was the runt of the litter that no one wanted, so the friend had agreed to put it in the store. "No, we can't," I said. "But look," he said, "it's talking to me." The woman feeding the snakes brought out the kitten for us, and it was clear there was little choice in the matter.

TJ and I had been living together for less than a year, having moved to Providence, Rhode Island on a whim. We had met in graduate school in Ann Arbor. As we were finishing our degrees, I said, "I'm thinking of moving to Rhode Island." TJ simply answered, "I'll come with you." Now we were both doing adjunct teaching with no plans for the future. Getting a cat together didn't seem like a smart decision, but that's precisely what we did as we paid our $8.00 and walked out with a kitten.

When we arrived back in our apartment, we watched as the kitten walked from one room to the other, taking his time as if he were considering purchasing a new home. After his tour, he settled firmly in a sunny spot in the middle of the dining room, letting us know that this was acceptable to him. Clearly he was the one who had chosen us.

For several days, while we bought cat food, a litter box, and bowls, we discussed what to name this new member of our household. TJ, who loved Jazz, suggested names like "Mingus" and "Parker." Looking at our confident gray striped tabby, I wasn't sure we should name him after anyone else. I was born in Egypt, so I searched for an Arabic word that might work, something like "Basboosa," but naming him after a pastry didn't seem right either. "How about Shango?" TJ said one day. "What's that?" I asked. "It's the African god of thunder and lightning." I looked at the kitten who was taking a leisurely walk around the dining room table in search of a good spot to lie down. TJ was African American and I was Egyptian. We were still in the early stages of our relationship, searching for that place where our cultures could meet. Shango was the right name.

Shango's personality emerged quickly and kept us on our toes. He hopped up on the kitchen counters scouring for food. He had a particular liking for cucumbers, peas, and banana bread, so leaving those on the counter was a definite risk. Shango's most annoying habit occurred at 5:30 every morning. He would hop up on our night tables and tap an item, like our eyeglasses or cups of water, slowly with his paw, moving them one inch at a time. If we didn't wake up quickly enough, they would end up on the floor. Several alarm clocks were broken that way as well as our two favorite coffee cups. At the time, we were still on our graduate school schedule, staying up late and waking up slowly in the mornings. We have Shango to thank for the fact that we are now both very early risers. His slow tap-tap at our bedside cured us of those leisurely mornings. However, Shango's most peculiar habit was jumping on top of the glass sliding bathtub door while TJ showered. There, Shango would crouch low to fit between the top of the door and the ceiling, balanced on the thin ledge like a tightrope walker, watching TJ take his shower.

A few months after Shango joined us, we were getting ready to go to TJ's parents for Christmas. Since we would be gone for just a few days, we simply planned on leaving enough food and water for him. We were packing in the living room, our open suitcase on the couch. Shango looked at us with what seemed to be an intention of inflicting guilt. "No," I said, "We can't take him with us. He'll knock everything down and break things." We weren't married yet, and this was our first overnight trip to TJ's parents' house. I didn't want to take any chances. "Right," said TJ, "Of course we can't." We ignored him and continued our packing. Then, hearing an odd noise, we looked up to see Shango coming out of the bedroom, dragging a canvas bag about twice his size in his mouth, which he promptly dropped at our feet. The message was clear. TJ called his parents, and they kindly extended an invitation to the feline member of our household. Shango was on his best behavior that Christmas. He didn't jump on the counters, and he didn't knock down a single cup. The only casualty was an ornament that accidentally broke as he was taking a walk around the Christmas tree.

When summer arrived, we began taking Shango outside. He loved being outdoors and would sit by the door meowing, as if he was uttering the magic words open sesame that would release him. When it was raining or snowing, we tried to tell him that he should stay indoors, but his perseverance was greater than ours. When we opened the door, he would see the rain pouring or the ground covered with snow, and then he would turn to look at us as if we had betrayed him. Still, he stepped out, only to return a few minutes later.

His first experience with another cat was when our friends asked us to take care of their cat, Coco. Coco was a large orange cat, limited to being indoors. It won't be too bad, we thought. After all, Shango was still young; he could adapt. He might even enjoy the company. But we had underestimated Shango's sense of ownership. He circled Coco, as if setting a trap for her hissed at her, and wouldn't let her out of his sight. One day as we were returning home, we saw Shango outside with a large orange cat. We panicked, not understanding how Coco could have gotten outside. Shango and the cat were playing with each other, locked in a tumbling embrace and rolling on the grass. But when we looked up to the window of our apartment, there was Coco, safely inside, watching the scene below. We had never seen this orange cat who was an exact twin to Coco, and we never saw him again. Clearly, Shango had won that round.

Little did we all know that Shango's exploration of the world had just begun. When I was offered a teaching job at The American University in Cairo, we made several phone calls and learned that yes, we could take our cat with us. We wanted to put him in a small container, so we could have him on the plane with us and place him under the seat. But he was too big now, his gray and white stripes giving him a prominent dignified appearance. He was no longer the runt of the litter; he had grown into the grand name we had bestowed on him. We had to opt for the larger crate and put him in with the luggage. After the twelve-hour flight, Shango emerged with the suitcases, his carrier turned upside down, meowing furiously.

As we walked through customs, I was called aside with Shango. We were ushered into a small room with two men. I handed over Shango's papers: proof of his vaccinations and the vet's statement assuring his good health. But the men had little interest in these documents. Instead, they proceeded to ask me when I had left Egypt and why. "America is a great country," they said. "Yes," I answered, "and so is Egypt." Why did I come back, they wanted to know. The pause that followed their question was a heavy one, and it seemed that my answer would either release us or hold us captive. It had been over twenty years since my family had emigrated and almost fifteen since my last visit as a child. "Because Egypt is my country," I answered. They smiled and nodded, handing me the papers they had not looked at and allowed Shango and I to step through customs. Twenty years after immigrating, it was Shango who ushered me back into my native country and introduced me to the political complexities of the relationship between East and West.

In Egypt, Shango was limited to being indoors, a change he did not take too well. We had to open and close doors carefully since his attempts to escape the confines of the apartment were constant. We were on the top floor of the building. Right above us was the large enclosed flat rooftop, which Shango discovered on one of his successful escape attempts. It was filled with assorted items for him to explore. It was also where the stray cats came to find a resting place from their wanderings. That is where we met a small cat we named Oliver, a tabby like Shango but with brown and white stripes. Shango seemed to like Oliver and once or twice actually let him eat out of his food bowl. We tried to tame Oliver, hoping to adopt him, but after we squirted him with flea and tick spray, he stayed away from us.

Shango made other feline friends, crossing the cultural boundaries with ease. A few times, he snuck out for greater explorations, perhaps learning more about Egypt than we did. After three years, we returned home. Shango survived the airplane ride, but I'm not sure he ever forgave us for his adventure in Egypt.

We returned to a new location, Binghamton, New York, carrying not only Shango, but also our first daughter, Yasmine, who was born in Egypt just a week earlier. As we settled into graduate housing at the university where both of us were about to begin the Ph.D. program, we quickly learned that no pets were allowed. We tried to explain this to Shango. He would have to stay indoors and keep a low profile, so he could stay with us. We also began to hear horror stories about how cats react to the arrival of children in their households. "Keep him away from the baby," everyone said. We took some precautions, careful not to leave Shango alone with our daughter, but after a few sniffs, Shango put his tail up in the air and walked away. He decided to ignore the arrival of this new creature, yet we could tell he was not pleased to be pushed aside from his position as the center of our attention.

Unfortunately, our low profile lecture had little effect. Shango spent his days sitting by the living room window, where anyone walking by could get a clear view of him. It wasn't long before we were sent a warning. We were lucky to find David, a fellow graduate student living off campus, who was willing to take Shango in for a while. David also offered the advantage of teaching Shango some social skills since he had two other cats. We knew Shango was in good hands, and soon David began telling us stories of his escapades. He surprised us by living peacefully with the other two cats, which meant he was willing to ignore them. Shango developed one unique skill while living with David. He began to follow him. When David walked to the store, Shango trotted right behind him. He waited outside as David shopped then followed him home. Once, Shango went missing for the whole day. It was getting dark and David still couldn't find him. David retraced his steps. That morning he had gone to the store, so he returned, and sure enough there was Shango sitting dutifully outside the door. Apparently he had not seen David come out and had waited all day.

After a year, we moved off campus, and Shango returned to live with us. He settled in and claimed his space. Quickly, he came to know his new neighborhood. Within a few days, our next door neighbor, a woman from New Zealand, was knocking on our door, asking if that was our cat. She complimented his beauty and his manners, asking if it was ok to leave food out for him. A little later, the older woman across the street, who always complained about people parking in front of her house, came over to introduce herself and ask about our nice cat. Shango made friends faster than we did, and, with his help, we soon found ourselves settled comfortably among our new neighbors.

A few years later, our second daughter, Celine, was born. Shango showed little reaction, again sniffing the new presence and going about his business. But he began spending less time at home. Instead, he wandered around the new neighborhood and soon acquired a reputation among the other cats as a fearless leader. He took on any cat and claimed his ownership of the entire neighborhood.

Shango's travels weren't over yet. When TJ and I finished our degrees, we headed to Roanoke, Virginia where TJ had been offered a job at Hollins University. The movers came and carried off our belongings. With nothing left in our apartment, we got into the car. I sat in the back seat with our two daughters, and Shango sat in his carrier in the front passenger seat. He kept up a steady meow that remains our strongest memory of that trip.

We moved into faculty housing, and Shango now had an entire campus to call his own. As usual, it didn't take him long to stake out his surroundings. We came to know our neighbors very quickly as they stopped to ask if that was our cat they saw walking down the middle of Faculty Ave., or wandering around the parking lot, or asleep on top of their car.

At times, we would get a phone call from a concerned student to tell us she had seen Shango over by the campus post office. The lessons he had learned from his time with David remained, and he had the habit of following us. If we didn't watch for him as we headed home, he might end up staying where he saw us going into a building. TJ began to sneak out the back door of our house in the hopes that Shango wouldn't notice his departure. Perhaps he feared that being seen with a cat following him would jeopardize his new position.

At times Shango brought us presents: t-shirts, towels, and assorted pieces of clothing that he apparently gathered from the neighbor's yards. It was a great source of embarrassment to us. We had to guess which house the item came from and then sneak back when no one was there to return it.

Shango acquired a particular fondness for the people who lived next door regardless of who they were. Something about that house attracted him or maybe he just wanted us to be jealous of his attentions to others. We went through three sets of neighbors, and, each time, he made himself likeable enough that they began to let him in and feed him. We heard stories of how he curled up and snuggled on their laps, something he never did with us. He grew particularly attached to our third set of neighbors. Walking into their house just a few months after they moved in, we saw two cat bowls in their kitchen. "They're for Shango," they explained.

When their daughter was born, Shango was no longer allowed inside their house. As I walked home, I would see Shango sitting on the air conditioner outside their kitchen window, peering in, clearly devastated by no longer being the center of their attention.

Perhaps Shango's greatest obstacle came about two years after we had moved. A dog had wandered on campus: hair matted, skinny, and with a collar taped to a cut-off chain on his neck. We petted him and gave him some food and water. We admired his sad eyes and what appeared to be his Border Collie and Australian Shepherd mix. "No, No," we said, "There's no way we can handle a dog." But the next day, when I opened the back door to find that he had slept there the whole night, it was clear that once again we had been chosen. Our older daughter named him Zak, and we took him to the vet and the groomer for a thorough cleaning. Then came the test of how he and Shango would get along. Zak made gestures of friendliness, approaching

Shango and sniffing him, but he was met with an arched back and a strong hissing every time. This went on for about a week until one day, Zak stood his ground and started barking at Shango, who meowed back. This barking and meowing from the two corners of the room continued for about ten minutes, until it seemed a truce was called. From then on, Shango tolerated Zak.

But Shango spent more and more time outside, even in the rain and snow, refusing to come in. When we did force him inside, his high pitched whining meow drove us to let him out again.

We went to Egypt again for six months when TJ received a Fulbright, leaving Shango in the capable hands of the house sitter and the next door neighbors. We knew he didn't want to experience another cross-Atlantic flight. I wasn't sure he would still be there when we returned, but as we entered the house after our long journey, there he was asking for food as if we had been gone only a day. Although he managed to stay out of trouble for those six months, within a few weeks of our return, he got into a fight and we had to take him to the vet. He needed an operation and special medication. The vet also discovered that he had feline aids, which he might have gotten from the cat that bit him. We were told he would probably lose his appetite and might not last more than a few months.

Shango was about thirteen years old at the time, and in true Shango fashion, he didn't lose his appetite. Instead it seemed to increase, and he insisted on two cans of food for breakfast every morning. About six months later, our neighbor called to tell us that Shango appeared to have gotten into another fight and didn't look well. So back he went to the vet for another operation and more medicine. The vet warned that as long as we let him go outside, he would get into more fights. To keep him safe, we had to make him stay indoors. But Shango's persistent meowing tried our patience. He stood by every door waiting to dash out the minute somebody opened it. We could keep him inside safe and miserable or we could let him out where no doubt he would get into another fight, but he would be happy.

He had already outlived the vet's dire prediction, and we were sure he would live forever. Apparently he had been blessed with more than the usual nine lives. Shango was now fifteen years old, still wandering around the campus with his tail up in the air.

Spring arrived and Shango began hunting rabbits. Apparently the two cans of food were insufficient. It was the beginning of August and Shango had been gone for two days, which wasn't that unusual. Still, we were concerned and kept an eye out for him. As I was walking back from the office on another hot and humid day, I cut across the yard, hoping to get home a few steps quicker. Behind a bush at the edge of the house, I heard a cawing sound like a hawk. Immediately I knew it was Shango. "Shango," I said, and he meowed back. We went back and forth a few times. Again, Shango was talking to us. I ran to get TJ We got him out from behind the bush. He was clearly dehydrated, had lost a lot of weight, and seemed very weak. We took him home and gave him water, which he drank, but he wouldn't eat anything. He refused the towel we tried to put him on, instead staying on the cool concrete floor in the basement. We took turns petting him, and his purring reassured us a little.

"Perhaps he's just dehydrated from the heat," we said, but I knew from the way he had called out to me that he wasn't likely to make it. We planned to take him to the vet in the morning. When TJ woke up early to check on him, Shango still lay curled on the floor and didn't even turn to look at him. A little later, Yasmine woke up and went downstairs. She came back to say he was breathing funny and loud. TJ went down five minutes later and came up to tell us that he had died. Shango lay curled in sleeping position on the floor as if he were just resting.

In his last years, we had begun to doubt Shango's loyalty to us as he seemed to prefer the company of our neighbors. But in the end, he knew we were his family and he came home to die. The day he died, it rained for the first time in two weeks and the wind picked up, swaying the trees and darkening the sky. He lived up to the name we had given him. We buried him in the backyard and put up a gravestone that says, "Shango, God of Thunder and Lightning, and our beloved cat."

The Artistry of Circumstance

M Y FATHER-IN-LAW IS FOND OF USING THE TERM, "the artistry of circumstance," to refer to those times when certain events combine to create an occurrence of almost supernatural good fortune. He ascribes the term to M.B. Tolson, who was his colleague at Langston University in Oklahoma in the late 1950s. I prefer to believe that I'm in control of my destiny, that my meticulous planning and careful work is what creates those moments of good fortune.

***

When I returned home after graduating from Clark University in 1983, I planned on finding a job and saving enough money so I could lead a more independent life. My parents had a slightly different plan: they had already lined up potential suitors and determined that I would get a job at a company that would pay for me to get my MBA in the evenings. In college, I had double-majored in English and Business. The Business was intended to appease my parents and ensure that they continue to pay tuition. I ended up with a part-time job at a small publishing company, making little money and wondering how I would ever achieve economic independence. I felt my future slipping out of my hands. If I didn't find a way out, I would end up working in an office, getting my MBA, and marrying an Egyptian doctor.

During my last year of college, I had briefly dated someone who was getting his MA in English. When I asked him what that involved, he answered nonchalantly, "You read more books and write more papers." That was good enough for me. Within a few months after returning home, I was already navigating my way through graduate school applications. There is some advantage to being oblivious to your own ignorance. I plowed ahead, taking the necessary exams, filling out forms, and writing essays.

Feeling conflicted about remaining close to home or moving further away, I decided to apply to a number of nearby schools, and then I added applications to the University of Michigan and the University of Chicago. I had heard that these schools had great English departments but knew little about them. I doubt I could have even located them on a map. Every school rejected me except for two—Michigan and Chicago.

Neither college offered financial aid. I polled my friends, but views were mixed, creating a split vote. Two factors ultimately guided my decision: money and landscape. Everyone said Ann Arbor was the cheaper place to live. Those who tried to dissuade me from going there described it as flat—"it's all corn fields," they said. The image of land stretching out in even plains, allowing one to see far into the distance appealed to me. Growing up in a Boston suburb, my walk home from school felt like hiking up a mountain, an exercise I didn't enjoy especially in the winter when, even after several years of living in America, I still had not mastered the art of trudging through snow. On our last trip to Egypt, as our Nile cruise boat flowed past the fields of Luxor and Aswan, my eyes feasted across this land where you could stretch your vision into the far distance. I accepted the offer from Michigan.

***

On the first day of my American Literature class, as the professor took attendance, my attention was caught when he called out the name "Suhair." I heard a voice respond, "It's Lisa." I scanned the room trying to determine the source of this name. My eyes travelled from one face to the next. I stopped at a young woman with a head full of curly light brown hair, sharp blue eyes, and full lips. Her complexion was lighter in tone, but despite the fairness of her appearance, her Arab ethnicity was clear. The hair, the lips, and her direct gaze gave it away. I approached her after class and asked. "How did you know?" she responded in surprise. I must've said something like "it's obvious," before I considered whether she might be offended. Instead, she seemed pleased to have been recognized.

This began my friendship with Lisa Suhair Majaj. It was from Lisa, who had grown up primarily in Jordan with a Palestinian father and an American mother that I learned to understand the term Arab American with its political and cultural meanings. Having immigrated at the age of eight, I knew little about Arab politics and history. My conversations with Lisa began to fill in those gaps and helped me to configure the political dimensions of my identity. Being Egyptian, I realized, extended beyond knowing how to make grape leaves and being able to belly dance. I began to explore Arab and Arab American literature, and although my searches led only to a few books that were available at the time, it was these explorations and Lisa's guidance that reawakened my desire to write out of the immigrant/Egyptian experience.

My friendship with Lisa has traveled from Michigan to Massachusetts to Cyprus with occasional stops in Egypt, Paris, and Roanoke. Whenever Lisa and I get together, our conversations run marathons, and our husbands know that they will need to feed themselves, keep track of the children, and relinquish any thought of being on time. When we coincidently found ourselves in Paris during the same week, our husbands had to physically pull us apart so Lisa and her family could catch their train.

***

In my last year of the program, I decided to take a class on Jewish-American literature. Perhaps it was the hyphenated identity in the title that attracted me. This was the mid-1980s, and most of the classes I had taken focused on mainstream American and European literature.

It takes time to sharpen our vision and look back to recognize those moments that pivot our life's direction. For me it was Professor Anita Norich's Jewish-American Literature class. For the first time, I read books that held a strand to my own life. *Call it Sleep* by Henry Roth, the saga of an immigrant family floundering to recreate their lives in a new world, initiated my own process of raveling and unraveling the threads that had created my identity as a young Egyptian immigrant. I responded to the deep sense of loss and longing in *The Assistant* by Bernard Malamud with an intuitive sense of recognition. It was Anita Norich's ability to lay this literature in front of our eyes and reveal its layers of intricacies that seeped inside me. She focused on the critical analysis of the work, but a side comment or a slight personal reference made it clear that she held a deeper relationship to this literature. Hers was not the distant gaze of a scientist studying an unfamiliar object under a microscope. Rather, it was the knowledge of the reality that lay beneath the words on the page, which enabled her to analyze this literature in a way that brought us closer to its most intimate meaning.

My vision of who I wanted to be developed into a parallel image. I imagined myself teaching Arab American and Immigrant Literature, working from the concentric circles of my own experience to bring an educated understanding to the study of this literature.

***

There was one more encounter at the University of Michigan that turned the axis of my future. As I scanned the classroom on that first day of Jewish-American literature, curious about the other students, my eyes stopped at a young man sitting on one end of the room, his long legs stretched out and crossed under the table. Something about him made me pause—his laid back attitude, the brown tone of his skin, the easy smile he displayed. That was TJ Anderson III, the man I would eventually marry. He was working on his MFA in Creative Writing, and I marveled at his firm identity as a poet.

The path that had led TJ to that Jewish-American Literature class was quite different from my carefully crafted one. When I met TJ, he gave full credit for his good fortune to his lucky star. My look of skepticism did little to dissuade him from his beliefs. Shortly before finishing college, TJ attended the Bread Loaf Writers Conference. The original writer who had been assigned for his one-on-one critique was unable to be there, and he was re-assigned to a different person. That was Richard Tillinghast, who was impressed with TJ's work and asked about his future plans. Seeing that he didn't have any, he suggested to TJ that he apply to the MFA program at the University of Michigan, where he was teaching. While I had struggled with my multiple applications, TJ had applied to one school. Somehow our incongruent paths intersected, and they continue to guide us—a careful plan combined with chance creating the pattern of our lives.

***

Two of my closest friends at Michigan were Amr and Yasser, both of whom were international students from Egypt studying architecture. As the only Egyptian in my elementary school, middle school, high school, and college, I had learned to adapt to my isolation. These new friendships offered me an alternative supportive community.

My new friends were perhaps as intrigued by my Egyptian American identity as I was by their more clearly delineated Egyptian identities. It was Yasser who once told me that when I switched from speaking English to speaking Arabic, my entire self transformed—my tone of voice, gestures, body movements—"you become a different person with each language," he said. And as I wondered about my relationship with TJ, trying to understand what it would mean for me to marry someone who was African American, it was Yasser who laughed and pointed out that TJ had the looks of a typical Egyptian. "You come all the way to America," he said, "and you pick the most

Egyptian looking man you can find." It was also through the many conversations with Amr about the longing for home that made me realize I needed to go back to Egypt, ultimately giving me the courage to apply for the job at the American University in Cairo. Their friendship forced me to question where I had lost my Egyptianess and where I had chosen to become American—exploring that in between place of identity and cultural belonging.

***

TJ and I were recently invited to give a reading at the University of Michigan. In Ann Arbor, we showed our daughters where we used to live, pointing to TJ's attic apartment and my second floor apartment just on the edge of campus. We took them to Blimpies, the famous hamburger place where we were fond of ordering hamburgers multilayered with toppings. And we insisted they try fragels, deep fried bagels, an Ann Arbor specialty. The fact that we now order veggie burgers and our stomachs can't handle the heavy taste of fried food didn't deter us. We ended up at the park, a few minutes from campus, and piled the four of us into a canoe to recreate one of our favorite outings. It was an inexpensive afternoon when we lived on graduate school stipends—renting a canoe and paddling around the lake to watch the fish spawning, catch a glimpse of a turtle lying in the sun, or explore an unexpected turn in the lake.

There are moments when your life pivots on an axis turning you in the direction of your path. That moment for me was a place, an unexpected location where each person I encountered was a magnet of energy that propelled me forward. This could neither be planned nor anticipated—it can only be explained as the artistry of circumstance.

Movements

OUR MOVE FROM ANN ARBOR, Michigan to Providence, Rhode Island was sustained by borrowed money and an abundance of faith. My boyfriend, TJ, and I packed up our 500 dollar blue Mercury Zephyr, bought from a woman who assured us it was a good car although she "wouldn't drive it cross-country." So we loaded it up with our accumulated belongings and drove it from the Midwest to the East Coast, making the trip twice, the second time with a basketball on my lap.

We dropped our stuff at TJ's parents' house in Boston and made the trip to Providence in search of an apartment. My unrealistic desire for the ideal home combined with TJ's impatience along with our lack of money led us to signing a lease for the least expensive apartment we saw the first day. We were still a young couple, before marriage, children, credit card debt, and student loans would catch up with us. Having just finished our Masters degrees, our future remained hidden behind a curtain, and we could not know that this first move together would lead to others across oceans and continents. Our cultural backgrounds—African American and Egyptian—drew us to the neighborhood of this particular apartment. The Cape Verdean landlady along with the ethnic diversity of the neighborhood reeled in TJ's desire to "live with the people." In the early 70s, his family had moved to an affluent Boston suburb. As one of the first African American families to buy a house in the area, their initial adjustment was tenuous, marked by the racial slurs scrawled across their property. Having spent his high school and college years there, he was now searching for an alternative location where he could place himself. For me, the 400 dollar rent was the most I could imagine paying out of our empty wallets. We never noticed that the only source of heat came from an electric stove in the kitchen or that the front room was closed off or that the landlady's son seemed a little suspicious.

It wasn't until winter arrived, the cold chills coming in through the poorly insulated windows, that we realized there was no heat in the apartment other than what was produced by that electric stove, which offered about as much warmth as a space heater. By then, we had already been reprimanded for picking up our own mail—since the front room of the apartment was used by the landlady for storage, we were not allowed access to the front door where the mail was delivered. The landlady assured us she would give us our mail. Frustrated, particularly as we were both writers and dependent on the hope of acceptance letters for our creative survival, we started sneaking out to grab our mail when she wasn't home.

Our expectation of living in a diverse neighborhood seemed unattainable as our encounters with neighbors remained limited to hearing heightened voices arguing through the two feet of space between houses that blocked sunlight but allowed the most intimate details of people's lives to permeate through the thin walls. Hardly anyone said hello to us on the street, and no one knocked on our door to introduce themselves. We wondered if word got around that we were college teachers and so perhaps we were perceived as not belonging despite our dire financial circumstances. We were both teaching as adjunct professors—a fancy word for low pay and no benefits. Along with other adjuncts, we worked at several colleges, driving back and forth to teach multiple sections of introductory level courses that full-time professors preferred to avoid. One university informed us that we would only be paid at the end of the semester. Desperate and faced with the impossibility of living on nothing for four months, I drew up a petition and gathered signatures to present to the Dean in order to get the college to start paying its adjuncts on a monthly basis. Although our financial situation matched our neighborhood, I never felt at ease. Even carrying the laundry back and forth to the laundromat, the stares from neighbors seemed to set me in a closed frame.

We lived only a few blocks from Brown University and Rhode Island School of Design, but our neighborhood was far removed from these ivy towers. Hope High school was around the corner, attracting a less privileged student body, and we heard that the teachers had become so frustrated at students not doing their homework that a decision was made to simply stop assigning homework.

We adjusted to our isolation and spent the majority of our time in the small side room of our apartment where we had placed the computer, keeping the shades drawn. It was 1988, and our purchase of this first computer was a sign of our attempt at entering the professional world of academia. I prepared copious teaching notes on it, wary of being unprepared when I was barely older than my students, and in spare moments, I struggled through the writing of stories and poems. Occasionally, the landlady's son knocked on the back door because he had forgotten his keys and needed to cut through our apartment to get upstairs. We let him in, thinking we were doing a good deed. He was perhaps fifteen or sixteen, a bit sullen, mumbling his words in an undertone. We deciphered his request to walk through our apartment more by his appearance at our back door than by anything he said.

One day, returning from visiting family in Boston, we stopped to pick up some Chinese food for dinner. That allowed whoever broke into our apartment enough time to take our computer, printer, and scrounge through the top drawer of my dresser to find the small tape recorder and a pair of earrings but not quite enough time to come back for the stereo left in the middle of the living room, its wire wrapped in a tangle.

When I walked in, my eyes blinking to the slight readjustment of objects, I didn't realize what had happened until I stepped into the small side room and saw the square dust pattern on the makeshift desk where the computer had been. My inside dropped like an elevator with its cables snapping. The landlady's partner came in with panting breath to tell us she couldn't catch him, that she had tried, that she knew it was him. The landlady denied it. Over the next few days, pieces of information buzzed around us…her older son was in jail…this younger one was on probation for something…the woman across the street had been robbed three times. This theft wove us into the neighborhood, and people approached us to ask questions, give condolences, or share their own story. The barriers that had kept us strapped as outsiders broke loose, and we entered the neighborhood.

We had no record of serial numbers, no rental insurance, nothing to compensate us for our naiveté. TJ drove from one pawn shop to the next, browsing through discarded, lost, and stolen items in hopes of finding our things, but his search led to nothing. I was fearful every day as I opened the door. Our wavering decision to move was made the night we watched two young men jump through the window of our next door neighbor's apartment; the tenants had never bought shades and their rooms sat exposed to the neighborhood.

We chose an apartment on the other side of town, complete with heat, our own mailbox, and extra rooms in the attic that we could use as studies. This was clearly an upper-class neighborhood with mostly single family homes and well-kept yards. Yet, we hesitated, uncertain of moving into this more elite section of the city, wondering if perhaps we didn't belong there. Whatever mathematical calculations I attempted didn't add up to affording the 700 dollar monthly rent plus utilities, but we still signed the lease. Perhaps we took that leap of faith because the landlord was a Russian immigrant. There was no doubt he was a shrewd businessman, but in the tone of his accent, I heard our shared immigrant history and believed he would negotiate with some kindness. We moved into our unfurnished apartment, retrieving TJ's bed from his parents' house, scattering a few pillows to create a living room, and configuring our milk crates into a dining table. We were no longer with "the people," but the initial lack of friendliness seemed to stretch evenly across town.

Our next door neighbor was an older man who spent winters in Florida. Once fall arrived and the leaves began to cover the ground, he came out to rake. He gathered the leaves and tossed them over to our front yard. Perplexed, we asked why he was doing this; he leaned his body into the rake and strained his face forward to make the firm claim that the leaves came from our trees, blown over by the wind to his yard. His accusation intimated that we were responsible for the direction of the wind and the resultant displacement of these leaves. Initially, we thought his behavior toward us might be racially motivated, so we sought the help of our neighbors who lived in the down-stairs apartment. They were a young couple from Minnesota—two of the nicest people we had encountered—surely they would win him over. We watched our neighbor as he approached the old man and extended his hand. The old man glared at him, re-affirmed his claim that the leaves came from our trees, and left our neighbor's hand suspended mid-air. We could only conclude that some people are just indiscriminately mean to everyone.

A few weeks after we moved in, a young girl, maybe ten or eleven, approached us while we were raking those leaves. She introduced herself as living across the street and proceeded to give us a verbal tour of the neigh-borhood: "The people who used to live here were black—they came from South Africa—but I wasn't allowed to play with their kids; we live across the street—we're Jewish, the people next door are Catholic, what are you?" I looked at this young girl who had confined the world into such strict catego-ries and considered my options for a response. I could explain the complexity of our multiple identities, give the simpler answer of African American, or even select a regional definition. "We're Arab," I said, perhaps as an invitation to see beyond the barriers of labels. Her silence was followed by a retreat back across the street to her home, and that seemed to conclude our prospects of neighborly relations.

We lived in this neighborhood for a year, our contact with neighbors as limited as it was in the previous neighborhood. The girl's father across the street came over once to introduce himself although the mother never looked in our direction. And the old man continued to rake his leaves onto our front lawn. We enjoyed our apartment for the year we lived there and learned to exist within the precarious boundaries demanded by the perception of our identities.

Among Neighbors

OUR NEIGHBOR GRILLS MOST SUMMER EVENINGS, even when rain threatens to cool the fire and pour on the picnic table set up in the middle of the driveway that he shares with his neighbors on the other side. The first summer we moved in, I'd watch out the kitchen window as he stood in front of his large gas grill, the cover propped open so he could turn whatever he was cooking with the long fork. David was tall with black hair and strongly accented cheekbones. In the summer, he wore jeans—often we'd see a row of them hanging on the clothesline—and no shirt, his slender body at ease with the sun and breeze of summer days. He moved with an air of calmness as if he were simply part of the changing seasons. Often, he'd stroll away from the grill to smoke a cigarette. It was a ritual that seemed integral to his life. "They're barbecuing again," I'd say to my husband, who preferred to keep the shades pulled down so no one could see us at our kitchen table as we ate.

When a young couple moved into the house next door on the other side of our neighbor, it wasn't long before they were barbecuing together, and that is when the picnic table was set up in their mutual driveway. "Well, no one ever invites us," I pouted to my husband, who responded with a flat hum. But maybe it's the nature of sharing a fence—soon my husband and David began to talk, and it was they, rather than David's wife and I, who began the relationship. We'd been there over a year, and perhaps that made us less threatening to them and the other neighbors since they realized we weren't the usual transient students. After spending three years in Egypt, teaching at the American University in Cairo, my husband and I had moved to Binghamton to attend graduate school. Maybe knowing we were going to stay for a few years made us feel courageous enough to speak to those with whom we shared the street. From the kitchen, I'd hear David and my husband talking. Fortunately, they were both tall and had to crane their necks only slightly to see over the gray wood fence.

"What were you talking about?" I'd ask. Usually, the response was "nothing," but occasionally I'd get a tidbit of information: his wife's name is Emma and she's getting a degree in social work; he watches the weather channel; his father left the family when he was young.

Emma seemed more aloof, her lips thin and set firmly in place. I suspected she was the one who did most of the worrying in the family. As we tried to see each other over the bushes, it was difficult to find a topic for conversation, or maybe women just have a harder time chatting in that casual manner that men adopt so easily. Then Emma got pregnant and their first daughter was born. We went over with our daughter, Yasmine, who was two years old to offer congratulations and found common ground as we talked about children.

When the next summer arrived, David started gardening, and soon we found large zucchinis balanced on the fence for us. One day, I returned home to find that we had our own makeshift garden created by my husband and daughter. David had offered snippets of his own plants to get us started. The herbs survived, but the strawberries eventually became food for the squirrels.

After a few initial skirmishes, our cats learned to get along. Once, I saw David's black and white cat, Casey, and our gray tiger cat, Shango, sitting on opposite ends of our front porch, eyeing each other. Perhaps that was the moment of their truce. After that, I would often glimpse Casey strolling through our yard or even coming up to the back porch as if he were waiting for Shango to come out and play.

We slowly learned about our other neighbors. Mrs. Smith, who lived across the street, was in her eighties; she was a thin woman who still dressed carefully and went to the beauty parlor. Two things preoccupied her attention: the snow and parking. We quickly figured out that to qualify as good neighbors, we had only to respect what she considered to be her parking spot, which was directly in front of her house. As long as her spot remained reserved, we were praised as ideal neighbors and also subjected to stories about others who had lived in our apartment and violated the sacred laws, either by using her spot or neglecting the alternate street parking in the winter months. I watched in amazement as she shoveled out her own car during the winter and swept her stairs in the summer. On Christmas and Easter, she came by to offer candy to our children. She also made sure to let us know when garbage pick-up day was changed due to a holiday. We dubbed her the watchperson of the neighborhood.

Mrs. Sweeney, next door to us, also came over with small presents for the kids on holidays. I was amazed she could think of anyone else when she had nine grown children and numerous grandchildren of her own. She was a short woman with white hair that rested slightly on her shoulders. Something about her seemed rounded out, as if all the hard edges had lost their sharpness through the years. She spoke with a slight accent that sounded partly British, partly Australian—I think once she said she was from New Zealand. Our relationship began when her husband came over one day to introduce himself to my husband, making a point of informing him that he had a son-in-law who was black. Mr. Sweeney was an older man, tall and well-built, usually wearing a baseball cap. He had spent many years in the Marines, but it wasn't until after he died that we found out he had been a school principal after he retired from the military.

Soon after Emma gave birth to Caroline, I became pregnant with our second daughter, Celine. Then David and Emma's neighbor on the other side, Lori, got pregnant. So the jokes began about something in the water and how many times it would go around.

Two summers later, Caroline turned two and Emma had another baby, a little boy they named Ben; Yasmine was approaching five and Celine was a year and a half; and Lori's daughter, Genevieve, turned one. It was that summer that our children found each other.

Caroline and Yasmine began to play, and, as soon as the weather warmed, their playing took them to the backyard. They would crawl through the overgrown wild berry bush next to the fence into each other's yard. I would watch them, or David, who stayed home during the day, would keep an eye on them. But the barriers became annoying when Yasmine needed to use the bathroom or if Celine joined them because she had to be watched more carefully or if David had to go in and feed Ben. One afternoon, the sun finally relenting of its summer heat, the kids were running back and forth, and we all became a bit tired of stretching our necks over the fence. David began investigating the long poles on his side to see how the fence was put together. I nodded at his suggestion, and a few minutes later, a large section of the fence came down, carried away by David and my husband. Soon, our children were marking a path back and forth, claiming new territory.

David suggested a barbecue, and we compromised our varying dinner times to create a meal together. Between us, we had hamburgers, hot dogs, ribs, and chicken on the grill. Caroline ran back and forth to the picnic table and managed to consume almost the entire jar of pickles before we noticed. Celine sat herself in the center of the yard, the potato chip bowl firmly planted in her lap. If anyone dared to suggest she might want to share, they were given one of her lowered eyebrow squints and a sneer. The adults enjoyed the rest of the meal.

A few days later, standing in the kitchen wondering what nutritious, tasty dinner I could produce with turkey burgers, I looked out to see David standing by the grill. "Hey, David," I said without wondering if I was imposing, "Are you grilling tonight?" He nodded, so I asked if he had room for some burgers, and another communal dinner was on. When my husband returned, I announced we were eating with the neighbors again. His puzzled look subsided once he was outside, enjoying some male company with David and Lori's husband, Rick, instead of his all-female household.

Combined with David's spicy sausage and Rick and Lori's artichoke salad and barbecue beans, our burgers became part of a gourmet feast. And, with Rick's mother and his older daughters there, the child to adult ratio was in our favor as our children crawled and ran around the two yards. When the drizzle began, we ignored it and continued to eat. But when the raindrops grew louder and heavier, we covered the food, and our quick consultation over whose porch we should run to settled on Rick and Lori's, which was the closest. Everyone grabbed a plate, summoned a child, and we were off. Somehow, it was only the women and children who ended up on the porch while the men remained behind, presumably guarding the grill, although later I found them huddled on David's back porch. Soon Yasmine and one of Rick's older daughters were skipping up and down the steps, teasing the rain.

I wonder about this moment that rain, food, and children created. Had we met elsewhere, we probably would have never come to know each other. But sharing space can force an intimacy, stretching us beyond our seclusion. For me, that rainy evening was one of the rare moments when I felt located in one place, when cultural identity seemed superseded by being neighbors. At the end of that summer, we would move to Virginia. That evening, David, half-jokingly, said, "You'll find better neighbors and not even care about us anymore." Somehow I didn't think so. A friend who had grown up in Virginia had tried to reassure me recently about racial relations by telling me we probably wouldn't experience much direct discrimination, except maybe in housing.

The next day, David and Emma were not around. We used our own grill for a change and ate dinner alone. At the end of the evening, my husband tossed a few knots of sugarcane onto the still smoldering grill, and a sweet roasted smell spread over our neighborhood.

The Camel Caper

WHEN MY HUSBAND STEPPED OUT TO GET THE NEWSPAPER early that morning, I was sitting in my usual chair keeping watch on the sky, waiting for the sunrise to stretch its orange streaks against the trees and mountains. My thoughts were the inevitable end of semester panic—last day of classes, return papers, collect papers, pass out evaluations—and in the back of my mind there was the urgency of Christmas: presents, cards, bills, braving the mad traffic of the season, and our impending trip to spend the holiday with family. All of that dissipated when my husband re-entered, saying, "Someone stole...." My mind took a few seconds to shift its attention. When I heard "stole," I assumed it would be followed by newspaper, but the next word was "camel."

"No!" I screeched even though I was barely through with my first cup of coffee. Heading toward the front door, I opened it to see the sparkling lights strung up and around the thin trunk and branches of our single dogwood tree. "Whimsical," one neighbor had referred to it. No, we were not known for elaborate holiday decorations as much as my children would have liked. My husband and I were both English professors, and we had minimal talents in technical things. Our attempt to untangle lights each year led only to this rather absurd sculpture in our front yard. However, this season, we had made great leaps. I had bought a large plastic Christmas camel that lit up. Except now, as I peered into the early morning darkness, there was only an empty spot, barely an indentation in the ground to mark the camel's previous presence.

A few years ago, we had stopped to admire the extravagant decorations of a house whose front yard displayed the true Christmas spirit. We marveled at the Santa sleigh, the inflatable snowman, the giant light-up candy canes, the glowing nativity scene, and then I noticed the camel. There he was crouching next to the baby Jesus, his face lit up with joy, a small green blanket over his hump, and definitely a smile on his face. "A camel!" I shouted, and my family backed me up on this one—the camel was definitely very cool. I wanted one. After all, I was Egyptian. It made sense that I should have a camel in my front yard. And maybe one day, I could get the palm tree with sparkling lights I had recently seen in a store. But it was probably best to hold off on that. I didn't want to jeopardize my family's approval for the camel. I looked up again at the crowded yard. Forget the rest of the nativity scene—it was only the camel that mattered.

When you're an immigrant, certain things come to epitomize American culture for you, and for me one of those things was lawn ornaments. True Americans had inflatable pumpkins at Halloween, wobbling snowmen at Christmas, and for the rest of the year there were flamingos. Perhaps a camel was not exactly the same, but in my heart, I knew my camel was helping me to carve out a space for myself in this new world. Now it was gone.

How could they? How could someone take our camel? I was devastated, inconsolable. Even my husband acknowledged the meanness of this act. Here we are living on a college campus where it's supposed to be safe and someone takes our camel. This camel was my great accomplishment. I had wanted flamingos, but my usually obliging husband had drawn the line there and vetoed the flying pink birds. As American spokesperson in the family, he had declared the flamingos unacceptable. Yet recently, he had surprised me by suggesting that we should get four camels, one for each member in our family. Wow, I thought, now we're getting somewhere.

I ranted and raved all morning. Then, empowered by my daughters' fallen faces when I told them, or maybe it was their fear that this would send their mother off the deep end, I decided to calm my anger and take action. I sent my husband off to file a police report at Campus Security.

The woman taking down the information asked, "Was that the only thing taken from the nativity scene?"

"Ummm…there wasn't a nativity scene," my husband had to acknowledge.

"It's not part of a nativity scene?" she quizzed him again.

"It was just the camel," he answered, forced to clarify.

"Just a camel…how quaint," she said as she finished filling out the report.

Clearly we had to do something else. Surely the thief should have known better than to take a camel from an Arab. Such actions call for serious retaliation. Signs, I thought; if the camel is on campus, we'll embarrass the culprits into handing him back. I typed in large bold letters:

STOLEN
LARGE PLASTIC CHRISTMAS CAMEL
FROM THE FRONT YARD OF FACULTY AVE HOME
PLEASE RETURN TO CAMPUS SECURITY

I asked my work study student to hang up the fifty flyers as I explained the calamity of the situation to her. She obliged and soon signs fluttered from every doorway and bulletin board.

When I sadly told my first class the news, several students said there was a camel that fit the description sitting on the window in the second floor bathroom of their dormitory. However, it wasn't clear how long it had been there . . . still it was a lead; there was hope. In the next class, one student announced that she had already gone to campus security with information regarding the camel in the bathroom. Another student gave me detailed instructions on how to secure the camel to a plank of wood and stake it to the ground. She had experience in such matters, since as a child she and her friends would transport lawn ornaments from various houses and place them in someone's unsuspecting front yard. The chosen person would pull their shades open the next morning and, with blurry eyes, look out on an assortment of creatures. Now I could have handled something like that. If someone had taken my camel and left a ransom note, perhaps demanding a tray of baklava in exchange, I could have gone along and delivered the requested goods to release my camel from captivity. But taking the camel without leaving a trace was a cruel act.

I went through my day with a heavy heart. Camels are glorious animals, known for their intelligence and hard work, as well as some occasional grunting and spitting upon waking up. They traversed the desert carrying travelers and their goods across a landscape of moving sands, allowing one tribe to go from place to place and trade with others. I remember riding on a camel at the pyramids, coerced by its owner who assured me it was safe. I settled on the camel's back, and the camel heaved back to raise his front legs, sending me into a precarious angle, but before I could attempt to regain my balance, he heaved forward to raise his hind legs, threatening to drop my body from its high perch. I gained great respect for camels that day and vowed to keep my distance.

However, the dignity of my camel had clearly been compromised. It had been unceremoniously scooped up from its comfortable location and taken to unknown places, possibly an environment unsuited to its native habitat. I wanted to know who took it and why. One colleague expressed her sympathy at the loss of our camel and asked what I would do if I found out who did it.

"You could take them to honor court or even file a report," she suggested.

"No," I said, "I just want to talk to them."

My daughters heard me, and their dark eyes grew large with fear, knowing the torture this person would have to endure.

Other condolences were offered as word spread across campus, and by mid-afternoon, it was clear that everyone knew about the camel. "I didn't take it. I don't know anything about it," one colleague said when he saw my husband. Another offered a clue, mentioning that her dog had barked furiously late into the night.

After teaching, I returned to the office and called my husband.

"The camel is back," he told me over the phone, his voice lacking the excitement it should have carried with this statement.

"What!" I said. "The camel is back. You have the camel."

"Yes," he said, as if it were obvious, "the camel is right here."

"Are you sure it's ours?"

"Yes, it's ours."

My husband had been called by Campus Security to come and retrieve the camel. He carried it in his arms across campus as one student pointed and laughed, announcing that this was the funniest thing she had ever seen. My husband embarrasses quite easily, and clearly he felt that being forced into the position of camel carrier had diminished his status on campus.

But the camel had suffered greater humiliations. He had indeed been found on the window of the second floor bathroom of West Dormitory. How degrading, to be placed in such an uncivilized environment after having traveled across the continents of the world.

My husband quickly sent out an email announcing that the camel had been found, in the hopes of silencing the rising crescendo of conversation surrounding its disappearance. We received several congratulations, and I was pleased to know that others cared equally about the well-being of our handsome creature. "Wonderful news," one Faculty Ave resident wrote back, adding, "Did it come back with any Frankincense and Myrrh?"

My daughters were equally relieved to hear the news and see the camel sitting calmly in our hallway upon their return from school. We snapped a few pictures—just in case he was ever abducted again. Next time, the posted signs would display the photograph of our gracious animal so he could be easily identified.

Later that evening, my daughters and I took a walk down Faculty Avenue.

"Look," Yasmine said, pointing to the only other house on the street with decorations. "Can't we put lights like that on our bushes? They would look really nice."

I sympathized with her longing for the more traditional display, something that would not mark her family's alienation.

"Aren't we going to put the camel back outside?" asked Celine.

"Yes," I answered, "Of course we will. And maybe," I added, "we'll get more camels so we can have four in our yard."

Our walk lengthened as we continued past houses tucking themselves into the darkness, not yet willing to announce the approaching holiday.

"You know what would be better," I said, "We'll buy one for every house on the street and then there will be a caravan of camels that we can all follow to take us home.

The House is a Mess

THE HOUSE IS A MESS . . . AGAIN. Dining room piled in a mismatched assortment of items that escaped from Celine's backpack—her giant size paperback algebra book split evenly down its spine, the hardback biology book that teaches weight lifting along with the makeup of cells, and the companion pair of Spanish textbook and workbook that cling to one another. Next to the giant size binder that captures the abundance of loose papers, all in various modes of planning their escape from bondage, and the color coded notebooks for each class, there are the pencils, all unsharpened; the remains of the protractor, a casualty of having sunk to the bottom of the bag; and the origami dollar bills, left over from purchasing french fries for lunch. These items often traverse from the dining room to the kitchen table, requiring additional time and restraint from screaming to ensure that a surface is cleared so we can eat dinner.

After a friend walked into my home, took one look, and exclaimed, "Looks like your daughter's backpack exploded in the dining room!" I renewed my quest for cleanliness and order. I set up a table in the back room and offered it to my daughter as her own study area, hoping to reclaim the more public parts of the house. This only resulted in adding to the space her assortment of items occupied; now the books and papers travelled all the way from the dining room to the kitchen and to the back room. I also went to her room and cleaned off her desk, adding pencil holders, book ends, and desk organizers in order to entice her to work in her room. This too failed, resulting in the newly organized desk surface becoming a receptacle for the excess from her dresser—hair scrunchies, nail polish, earrings, and a rubber duck.

I anticipate the day Celine leaves for college, fantasizing about the time I will have to pursue my own interests since I will no longer be relegated to picking up the trail of clutter she leaves behind. I imagine waking up each morning to a clear kitchen table where I can sip a leisurely cup of coffee while reading the paper, where each evening I can set plates on the empty surface of the dining table. Outside my kitchen window, I can glimpse into the neighbor's house. They are an older couple, their children having moved out and settled into their own homes. I can see their dining room, and the table is always set with plates, silverware, and napkins, ready in expectation of a meal. As I view this perfect setting, I know that this order cannot be my life. It's too quiet and steady, implying a predictable rhythm of daily ritual.

My family's journey has taken too many twists and turns to give us this offering. We have lived in too many homes, carrying our belongings from place to place to find new locations for our lives. In the first apartment my husband and I occupied with our two daughters, our dining room quickly claimed the prize of becoming the play room. Barbie dolls joined us for dinner, and walking through the room inevitably resulted in a loud "Moo" coming from the stuffed cow in the corner. My attempts to contain the toys failed each time. Pulling one toy from the mountain tumbled the entire stack. Not even my labeled plastic containers succeeded in restricting the spread of musical instruments, stuffed animals, and puzzles across the rest of the house.

Now, in this home, the first one we have purchased, our motivation for cleanliness and order are inspired by the monthly mortgage we have to pay in order to occupy this space. Perhaps that's why my desire for neatness has been heightened. But each of my attempts is short-circuited by Celine's whirlwind entrance into the house. Before I can yell out to take her shoes off at the door, she has already traipsed through the dining room and into the kitchen with muddy sneakers. As she begins the story of her day with no prelude, I point menacingly at her feet only to be answered by a defiant kicking off of the shoes, which get tossed under the kitchen table, and I know they will remain there until I pick them up and put them on the rug by the front door allotted for that purpose.

My daughter's focus is immune to my nagging, and she continues her story, interspersed with philosophical ruminations. Neither the shoes nor the socks she leaves behind that wander from room to room in search of their rightful place detract her from the stories she needs to tell or the paper she is writing or the art project she is planning. Her mind focuses on something beyond this trail of clutter.

I think of my mother and her younger sister. My mother would arrive at her sister's house and find her sitting in her living room chair, her feet resting on an ottoman, drinking a cup of tea, oblivious to the surrounding clutter of toys, dishes, and clothes. Her meditative breath came with each sip of hot liquid, and neither the dust on the furniture nor the urgent need to vacuum could disturb this moment of harmony set aside from the repetition of daily chores. Apparently, my aunt had brought with her the ritual of tea from Egypt. There, drinking tea requires stopping long enough to slowly sip from the glass cup filled with warm liquid, sweetened with too many spoons of sugar and fresh mint. In a country that centers its day around the heavy afternoon meal followed by a siesta, such moments of quiet when daily cares can be pushed aside are possible. But in the new world of America, my mother scolded that cleanliness needed to come before rest. "How can you relax in the middle of all this," she reprimanded, waving her arms about the messy room in an attempt to negate my aunt's achievement of peace. "I can only rest once I've cleaned," my mother asserted with defiance. But I knew that rest came rarely to my mother, who seemed to be chasing the ghost of a home that existed only between the pages of the glossy magazines she flipped through quickly in the few minutes she allowed herself, a reprieve from the constant frenzy of cleaning. That look of contentment on my aunt's face remained as elusive for my mother as the perfectly ordered house to which she aspired.

I have no recollection of being a messy child, but perhaps I must take some responsibility for my mother's unsuccessful quest to create order and cleanliness in her home. My father insists that when I entered the house, I would toss my bag, my coat, and my shoes in random directions, letting them land wherever gravity pulled them. He claims that my scattered belongings created an obstacle course through the house. Frustrated, and concluding that somehow my behavior must be due to the negative influence of American culture, he asked one of his colleagues for advice. The man suggested that my father gather my stuff and throw it all down the stairs into the basement, assuring him that if he did so, I would never again make a mess. I can't recall if my father followed this sage advice, but it seems the struggle against messiness has pursued me into adulthood. And perhaps this child of mine who squanders her belongings throughout the house is my parents' revenge for my own early behavior.

I constantly chase the accumulating clutter of my home, and it's rare that I stop to sit and rest. Too often, my cup of tea is snatched sips between mopping and laundry. I'm not sure if I aspire more to my aunt's happy obliviousness to the surrounding chaos or my mother's aspiration for an ideal home. There are times when I remember my aunt's pure contentment and I make that cup of tea, but to find that peace, I usually have to step outside and turn my back against the piles that gather in each room.

Perhaps my constant attempts to make my daughter collect her belongings and achieve order expresses only my envy of her ability to continue on her path, whether studying, reading, or drawing, without the mess nudging at her concentration. She has achieved a peace that I may have had as a child, but now I strive for it with rare success. At times, my sharp order to put away her laundry has been met with, "When I finish my cup of my tea." She and my aunt may have reached the highest level of meditation, in which the mind is at peace in the midst of chaos, while I'm still left stumbling over a pile of shoes as I enter my home.

Exchange 81

Route 81 became our pathway. We travelled almost the full length of it from Binghamton to the edge of Virginia, getting off to make our way to Chapel Hill. Those were graduate school years, both of us in school, arriving in Binghamton with our first daughter and then having our second daughter three years later. Each Christmas, we made our way south down the highway that we caught minutes from our rented duplex, our journey beginning in piles of snow and the frigid temperatures of winter in upstate New York. Our breath snagged on paralyzed branches as we snuck ourselves out of the house bundled in early morning. We transported suitcases and presents from home to car, finally carrying our daughters, still heavy in sleep into the sharp sting of cold and into the waiting car seat. I sat in the back with them while my husband navigated our way, following the direction of birds.

Going south, we knew we would find warmth. We travelled through a tiny bit of New York then the length of Pennsylvania, clouds forming a low covering to sky, still keeping the air chill and gray. Somewhere in Pennsylvania, we passed a sign that said "Blacks Run." Our imaginations brushed over those words: Was it a warning for runaway slaves or was it a sign of encouragement to keep heading north? Perhaps it was only the monotony of the winding road that made us wonder at the origins of those words and what they meant for us today—an African American/Arab American family heading south at the end of the Twentieth Century.

Finally, over the Mason Dixon Line, into Maryland, the sky lifts, letting sun emerge into light. By Virginia, we knew we had broken through frost and fog to arrive into the clear blue warmth that our skin craved. Our more than mid-way stop was Charlottesville where friends lived. Harlan had taught with us in Egypt at the American University in Cairo and his wife, Janice, was now a graduate student at the University of Virginia. They welcomed us in short sleeves with an overflowing bowl of pasta, along with a much-needed reprieve from the endless hum of the highway.

Christmas in North Carolina meant sunny walks and at least one unexpected day when the chill in the air retreated and allowed us to go out without jackets. We felt liberated as we wandered outdoors, the air and sun flushing our faces, reminding us of the joy that comes with unobstructed movement. At the end of the holiday, we became reluctant travelers as we made our way back up Route 81, keenly aware of the cold and snow that awaited us at the end of our journey.

After five years of Binghamton winters and long road trips, my husband applied to a number of jobs all across the country. We packed our books, the boxes piling up in our apartment ready to make yet another move. His job search led us back down the path of Route 81 to Hollins University in Roanoke, Virginia, a town whose signs we must have passed numerous times on our trips. We drove down the highway, along with our cat who complained in consistent meows as we made our way to our new destination.

Once we settled in this Blue Ridge Valley, a new location for our lives, I recognized its familiarity. *The Waltons*, which I had avidly watched as a child, took place somewhere within these mountains. That show tugged at me when I was growing up as a young immigrant in America, trying to make sense of this vast new world. Something about the natural landscape, different from anything I had known, appealed to me. I had grown up in the urban setting of Cairo, and we had settled in the suburbs of Boston. This environment with its green mountains and valleys held the appeal of a foreign land. But something about the large extended family on this show, all sharing a home, recalled my own family structure in Egypt. And the meddling in everyone's affairs also had a familiar ring. I dreamt of having this fantasized life in my future, complete with seven children.

For years as an adult I never spoke of my fondness for the show, recognizing the over idealized lifestyle it portrayed. Until, in passing conversation, my friend, Ursula, who had emigrated from Germany, mentioned it. We found our common ground. She too had watched the show avidly when she first arrived in America and was drawn into its storylines and characters. Perhaps it was the simplicity of how each problem was resolved that appealed to us, unlike our own immigrant lives that seemed wrapped in complex knots. In John-Boy, I saw a romantic version of my own desire to write and the family support I wished I had. Ursula recalled the constant refrain of "Good Nights," and perhaps the harmony of voices revealed her desire for an equally calm and loving family life. It seemed only just that the destiny of fate would lead us both to live so closely to the show's setting.

Over the years in Roanoke, our family found itself once again bound on Route 81, now heading north to make our way back to Binghamton to see friends and to Boston to visit my family. But we knew enough to limit these trips to the summer months. Among goats and chickens, we visited with our friends in Newark Valley, just outside Binghamton, professors who were also farmers, a world distant from our own background. We milked goats and harvested hay and learned that this lifestyle remained appealing for us only in our imagination. Then onto Boston to visit my parents and revel in family gatherings complete with stuffed grape leaves and ongoing arguments, accented by loud gestures and memories that faded into another country. Each time, we returned with a stuffed van, carrying all the things my parents offered us, assuring us that we needed them.

Our drive back south promised us lighter winters with gifts of sunny January days. We were fortunate to end up in the setting whose weather we had longed for on those winter trips, leaving behind years of shoveling snow and wearing summer clothes only for a few miserly weeks. The south was more generous with its sunshine, and these mountains that surrounded our valley protected us form the harshest storms.

Years later, our older daughter's college search led her to the least expected possibility from among the places she had applied, and we found ourselves heading back up 81 to drop her off at UVA. Once again, we retraced our paths. Our friends in Charlottesville had moved, and our trips there had stopped shortly after we came to Roanoke. But once again, 81 summoned us and we delivered our daughter to her unexpected destiny.

America is a vast country that stretches people across its borders. Our family's origins—African tribes insulated into cohesive communities and Egyptian villages with houses that expanded to accommodate children and their spouses—drew tight geographical lines that defined boundaries and kept families intact. In America, with its seemingly infinite possibilities, families fragment, and the roads travelled fade into an indecipherable pattern that can't be retraced.

Route 81 has circled our lives from Binghamton to Chapel Hill, from Roanoke back to Binghamton and to Boston, from Roanoke to Charlottes-ville. Each time we travel this highway, we wrap another thread around our lives tying us to people we keep close even through the distance of America's landscape. If we ever make another move, I know it will still be Route 81 that will take us there.

WITH CAUTION

Make It Like the Recipe

"Do you think nutmeg would taste good in this?" I ask, the question presumably directed to my husband since he's the only other person standing in the kitchen. I'm thinking about the pasta and broccoli with white sauce casserole I'm in the middle of making. It's a dish I've done before, but the original recipe calls for cauliflower. With the broccoli, I'm feeling a little suspicious of the spice's ability to add something tasteful to this time consuming concoction. But my husband's response tips the balance.

"Make it like the recipe," he says.

We've been married for twenty years, and this is what he has to offer in response.

"Make it like the recipe!" I shout back at him. "Well, perhaps you should just go have dinner at someone else's house. If you wanted me to follow the recipe then you should've married someone else. Maybe you should've married someone like your mother."

My retort is not intended with any meanness. On the contrary, perhaps it expresses my hidden jealousy. My cookbooks are filled with little index cards of recipes from my mother-in-law. They are handwritten and meticulously copied from their original sources. She gives them to me in response to my compliment of the dishes she serves us every time we visit. But when I pull out one of those cards to recreate one of her tasty dishes, I'm not able to follow her precise instructions. The one cup of rice edges its way to two, the teaspoon of cinnamon gets heaped up to come closer to one and a half, and I'm not so sure about having just mushrooms, so I add some asparagus. My mother-in-law is one of the kindest women I know. A harsh word never escapes her mouth, and she has been consistently supportive of all her children and their various endeavors. I continue to be amazed by her calm manner and ability to maintain an emotional equilibrium regardless of any turmoil that may arise. Unfortunately for my husband, he did not abide by the cliché of marrying a woman like his mother. He is now cowering in the corner of the kitchen, a panicked look on his face, perhaps because he knows he may not be served dinner tonight or perhaps because I'm waving a knife in my hand as I continue my rant.

"My mother doesn't follow recipes, my grandmother didn't follow recipes, and neither did my great-grandmother or any of the women before her—and no one would dare contradict their reputation for being excellent cooks. You don't like my cooking—fine, maybe you'd like a TV dinner for your meal, and you can eat it outside in a tent," I continue, brandishing my knife.

He shakes his head, trying to edge away from me. My husband knows better than to underestimate the wrath of an Egyptian woman, especially one holding a knife.

"If you wanted someone to make it like the recipe, you should've married an American." I add one more strike before turning my attention back to the simmering white sauce.

Having gained a few feet distance from me, he regains his confidence and responds with, "Let me see your passport—last time I checked you were an American."

I turn slowly from my thickening pot of sauce, the steam rising out of it. "I still have my Egyptian passport," I answer. "And if you don't like my cooking, I suggest you go find another home."

The glare in my eyes along with the aroma escaping from the pot of white sauce I'm guarding must have convinced him.

"I love your cooking," he vows with complete sincerity and crawls away to wait for his dinner.

Alongside my mother-in-law's careful index cards are the recipes I've inherited from my mother. They are scribbled in various notebooks and on slips of paper in my own awkward handwriting. Growing up, I became an avid reader, but my escape into the world of books was often disturbed by mother's voice rising up the stairs to summon me to come down and help her in the kitchen. I resented the interruption, but my mother's anger was not something I wanted to incur. I could pretend not to have heard a couple of times, but inevitably, the page had to be marked and the book laid down. In the kitchen, my mother's instructions to chop, peel, mix, and stir dominated the air. There were never any recipes, only my mother's trained hand guiding the process. But she was an extraordinary cook, and her food combined the tradition of Egyptian cooking with the imagination that had made her want to transform her life by emigrating even after she was married and had a child. There was always an unexpected flavor, something that made your tongue sparkle at the taste.

Despite all the help I was forced to offer in the kitchen, I didn't really learn to cook. My first desperate call to my mother happened in college. I had joined the Armenian club. There were no other Egyptians or even Middle Eastern students at my college, and this was the closest thing I could find. One of our main events was an International Dinner, and someone suggested I make baklava. "Sure," I said. I had helped my mother make it many times, and I certainly knew exactly what it should taste like. But as I considered the matter, I realized that I didn't actually know how to make it. Thus, the first panicked phone call to my mother. It took several calls as I struggled with the phyllo and the melting butter and the nut mixture to put this extravagant dessert I had always taken for granted together. Thankfully, it was a success and earned me the right to sustain my membership in the Armenian club.

My first escapade with the creation of baklava, monitored by phone calls to my mother, also led to my first scribbled recipe. After that, when I went home, I was less reluctant to help my mother in the kitchen. I brought a notebook with me and followed her movements, writing down her methods as she created the food I had grown up with, food that rarely existed outside the confines of our home. Phyllo with spinach, stuffed peppers and zucchini, pasta with ground beef and white sauce, grape leaves, okra with tomato sauce—I jotted down her ingredients and her methods, but there were no teaspoons or measuring cups in our home. My questions buzzed around the kitchen—*How much rice are you putting in? How many cups of water? How much garlic do you add? How many teaspoons of cumin?* But there was only some of this and a little of that, twice as much of this as that, and "taste it and you'll know," my mother said. I'd push her to reveal specific amounts and write them down as if they were sacred. But it took only one attempt at making the recipe with those amounts to know they were not precise. I was trying to gather information that could not exist in any quantitative terms. My mother cooked by taste, putting in a pinch of something, stirring and tasting and adding to get it right. I have evolved to become a cook by sight. When I add something, I look to measure the feel and texture and color until I know it's just right. Although I never taste anything until it has been set on the table, I have been known to glare at those who would dare add salt to my food, insinuating that I didn't get it right.

Following my mother around the kitchen garnered a notebook of hand-written recipes. That green hardbound notebook has now been splattered with drips of oil and butter from having it nearby as I attempt each of my stolen recipes. The binding has broken, and the book is held together by one of those thick purple rubber bands that circle the broccoli you buy in the supermarket. Each recipe has been modified since its first draft with alternate amounts written next to each ingredient and notes about other ingredients and substitutions I've made along the way. I suspect I'm creating an illegible legacy of culinary arts for my daughters who are only likely to peruse this book with confusion after I'm gone. But perhaps they will crave the food of their childhood—the *molekhia* soup that sends them into raptures of taste anticipation; the *koshari* that makes their eyes widen as the bowl of rice, lentils, spicy tomato sauce, and crisp fried onions is placed on the table; the grape leaves I have forced them to roll one by one in expectation of the aroma that seeps through the house until they're finally served with the garlic yogurt sauce; the spinach phyllo filled and wrapped into triangles that tempt them to eat just one more. These cravings will return to haunt their tongues, and they will flip the pages of this book to unearth some secret magic that can lead them back through generations of recipes that they will have to recreate and make their own.

It is a circular path that these recipes force us to take. Not long ago, my mother called, asking me to send her the recipe for the stuffed chicken she made one time when we were visiting. We liked it so much that once again I asked her how she had made it and wrote down what she told me. Later, during one of our phone calls when I mentioned making it, she remembered that she had also squeezed some lemon into the stuffing and added lemon zest. Those ingredients are still not included in the recipe I wrote down, and I'm forced to recall them each time I make it. Now she wants the recipe back, unable to reformulate its creation from her memory. I'll type it up, although her original recipe doesn't parallel how I make it. I've substituted ingredients to correspond to the likes and dislikes of my family members, creating something that only alludes to the original dish.

I have little patience with the precision of recipes and American cooking. The desire for consistency and replication that underlies this type of cooking doesn't correspond with my life, marked by my movement back and forth between two countries and a sense of home that remains unbalanced. Perhaps it's my winding life path that makes it so difficult for me to follow rules— there is always another way to get there even if it involves a lot of stumbling. This causes problems for my husband who spent four years in the Air Force, being indoctrinated into the hierarchical order of commands and rules that must be followed.

When I met him in graduate school, he had already failed the required French exam once. As he prepared to take it again, he received a sample test to study. Several times, I inquired if he had translated the sample test.

This question was usually answered with vague nods and a mumble about starting to work on it. When my husband sat for the test, he faced the exact passage that was on the sample he had received. Needless to say, the results of that exam were not positive. He continued in the program, meeting all the other degree requirements. As he was approaching the end, I inquired what he was going to do about the language requirement. A shrug of the shoulders and a mumble of "take it again I guess" is what I received. That summer, he was eligible to receive a fellowship if he took a class. With a lot of urging, I managed to get him to set up an independent study, translating the work of the French Caribbean poet, Aimé Césaire, whose work he had recently encountered. The independent study proved more rigorous than he had expected, but he produced strong translations of several poems.

"So, now what are you going to do about the language requirement?" I asked.

"Take the test again," he responded.

This time, I knew better than to just let him remain on his persistent path of failure.

"No, you're not," I countered.

He looked at me with alarm, sensing that I was about to suggest a plan that deviated from the set rules.

"You will submit a portfolio of the translations you've done along with a letter requesting that this independent study be accepted in lieu of the language test," I commanded.

His look of panic was followed by some stuttering and a string of "No—not what I'm supposed to do—can't break the rules."

I sat him down and stood over him as he typed the letter. Reluctantly and sheepishly, he submitted the request to the department. Only a week or so later, the response came approving his request, commending his work, and exclaiming that this was the true meaning of the language requirement.

Years later, our relationship still encounters those bumps as he walks solidly along the path that has already been established, while I zigzag around, occasionally tugging at him to take a different route. Maybe this is due to having come from such a bureaucratic culture where following the rules only earns you a headache and less than what you started out with. Egypt is known for its bureaucracy, its bribery, and the necessity of negotiating to get a fair price for anything. Only the clever who can navigate this system survive. Some cultural habits must be ingrained in you at birth, since I seem to continue to live by these methods even in an America that prides itself on its efficiency and fairness. But American culture is transforming, perhaps due to the flailing economy or the influence of immigrants arriving from places where negotiations maintain the equilibrium of the economic system. Most recently, while purchasing a rug for our home, my bargaining skills kicked in. After being given a price for the rug and the installation that was already lower than we anticipated, I asked if there was a possibility of an additional discount. My husband sat solidly next to me, although I knew he was trying to think of a getaway plan, some way of dissociating himself from my attempt to negotiate what he perceived as a set price. My request was met with an additional ten percent off.

All of this explains why I'm contemplating the use of nutmeg in my casserole that doesn't quite follow the recipe, while my husband is saying make it like the recipe. The nutmeg goes in and actually a little extra, especially since I've already almost doubled the amount of broccoli and tripled the amount of milk. I go on and add the black pepper the recipe doesn't call for. The brown and black spices get stirred into the sauce like a magic potion, swirling into a pattern that can't be replicated.

My Encounter with the FBI

I TEACH AT A SMALL UNIVERSITY where you get to know your students well, so naturally I'm asked to write a lot of recommendation letters and to serve as a reference when they apply for jobs. I'm happy to do it and usually it turns out just fine. This was the case, until a few years ago, when agreeing to serve as a reference led to some anxiety and also the urgent need to redecorate my office.

One of my students who recently graduated sends me an email telling me that she is applying for a position with the FBI and asks if I could be one of her references. I hesitate only for a moment. This is not the typical career my students seek out, but why not, I think, the FBI probably has lots of mundane jobs. "Sure, I'd be happy to," I answer in my usual manner.

A few weeks later, I receive another email from her, asking for my birth date, which she explains is required on the reference form. This time, I hesitate a little longer. I mark her email as unread and go home to discuss this with my husband. "That information is easily available," he says matter-of-factly, "Sure, give it to her, why not?" He's right. My birth date is not exactly a secret, and if you simply google my name, you'll find out far more than what the FBI wants to know, including the fact that three years ago, I painted a recycling bin on campus with my daughters. According to the newspaper article, our painting of an apartment building, mango and palm trees, and the Nile River represented my native land. The next day, I reply with the required information.

I forget about the FBI and resume my work. It's the end of the summer, and I'm preparing to teach my fall classes, a new course on Creative Nonfiction and Arab Women Writers, one of my more popular courses. The rest of my time is spent trying to get in touch with my co-editor, so we can finish the second edition of our anthology on Arab American Fiction. As usual, he's spending the summer in Egypt and Libya, so the possibility of getting an email from him is about as likely as finding a guava in my supermarket.

Then January arrives, our quiet month on campus. I'm teaching a four-week class on International Women's Films. It's late Thursday, and I'm in my office wrapping up for the long weekend. I do a final email check, glancing through the ones that have just come in. I see one from the FBI, but the jolt in my throat subsides quickly as I read enough of the preview lines to know it's about my student. Probably a reference form I have to fill out, I think. This time, I don't open the email, thinking it can wait until tomorrow or even Monday.

That evening, after returning home from taking my older daughter to piano lessons, my younger daughter greets me with, "Hi Mom, the FBI called you." I quickly make the connection to the email I didn't open. But then I think why are they calling me at home? Did I give them my home phone? And it is 7:00 in the evening, past normal business hours.

I go downstairs to find my husband in his basement hovel.

"I understand the FBI called," I say, trying to sound nonchalant.

"Yes," he answers, "it's about a reference for that student." Then he proceeds to tell me how when he made a mistake repeating the phone number the agent was giving him, the agent responded with "Negative."

"Negative?" I repeat.

"Yes," my husband confirms.

"Do I have to call him back tonight?" I ask.

"Yes, he's expecting you to call. Just do it," he says.

"You don't suppose," I say, "that this is all a scam and I'm actually the one being investigated, do you?"

Fortunately, my husband knows me well enough to know this is not a moment of insanity—just my typical paranoia. After all, I'm Egyptian, I teach courses on Arab literature, and I discuss Middle East politics in my classes.

"Professors have gotten into trouble for teaching these subjects," I remind him.

My husband soothes my fears, saying, "If they wanted you, they would've found you by now."

I brace myself as I head back upstairs and am met again by my younger daughter who just laughs and says, "Negative."

I think about our ongoing family joke. Whenever the kids are calling for me, demanding to know where Mom is, my husband says, "She's been deported." I use the same phrase when I don't want to be found. Suddenly my naturalized citizenship seems rather precarious. I announce to my two daughters that I'm about to call an FBI agent, and they have to be absolutely quiet—no whining, yelling, or arguing in the background.

The man on the other end answers the phone with "Special Investigator" before stating his name. Yet, he sounds more pleasant than I expected, and I'm a bit flustered. When he asks how I am, I answer "good" without going on to inquire how he is. I hear the pause and know I'm not off to a good start. The rest of the phone call is a fumbled attempt to set up an appointment to discuss my student on whom he is conducting a background investigation so she can receive a security clearance. Finally, we settle on meeting the next day in my office.

***

I get to my office two hours before the appointment. The first thing I see as I hang up my jacket on the back of the door is the Palestinian *keffiyeh* on the hook. This is not good, I think. I grab the scarf and tuck it into a file cabinet drawer. Then there is the pile of DVDs on my desk for the class I'm teaching—all international films including an Iranian film that happens to be on top. This could definitely be suspicious. Those go in the same drawer with the *keffiyeh*.

I look around more carefully now. My three books are displayed face front on one of the shelves: *Egyptian Compass, Letters from Cairo, Dinarzad's Children: An Anthology of Contemporary Arab American Fiction*. All questionable titles. My desire to show off my accomplishments quickly recedes, and all three books are tucked back into the shelf. Still their titles are clearly visible from the spines, and they are lined up next to books like *Post-Gibran Anthology, The Poetry of Arab Women*, and *Cultural Activisms*. Definitely not good. I move a picture of my two daughters and place it in front of the books and then put a vase with flowers next to it. I add a few other knickknacks. Much better, I think. Now you can barely make out the titles.

Then I notice the small stuffed orange camel hanging from one of the shelf hooks. Suddenly my fascination with camels doesn't seem so innocent. I try to weigh the relative danger of this stuffed animal. Medium, I think, and move it over so it's in a less visible location. Of course there is also the wooden camel on the windowsill that my husband gave me. I consider putting him away with the scarf and the films, but he looks rather content, staring out the window. I decide not to disturb him.

I stand where the agent will be sitting to consider his view of things. Right in his eye's vision is a postcard on my bulletin board advertising a film about gay Muslims called *A Jihad for Love*. Oh no, I think, as I snatch the postcard and tuck it under a pile of papers in the bottom desk drawer. Then I notice the old map leaning against the wall. Is that a map of Palestine? I wonder. Looking closer, I see that it is my map of North

Africa. Still, just to be on the safe side, it gets pushed behind the desk.

When I turn around, I'm faced immediately by the spine of a large book depicting Arabic words—my Arabic dictionary—and next to it several books on the grammar of the language. Arabic letters are always suspicious. I turn the dictionary around, so the pages are facing out then do the same with the nearby books. But when I step back, I realize that looks rather odd. I turn them around again. After all, the agent will have his back to these books—perhaps he won't notice them.

Another look around and my eye catches one of the folders on my desk with the word "Arabesques" written on it—another suspicious use of language. It's in reference to a conference at the Kennedy Center where I've been invited to be on a panel of Arab American writers. I slip the folder under another pile of papers on the desk. Now, I think I'm ready to meet the special investigator.

***

When he arrives exactly on time, I'm greeted by an older man: medium height, slightly heavy with gray hair and a friendly smile. I realize I had expected someone closer to the TV depiction of an FBI agent: someone tall, younger, and well-built, someone who could do a hundred push-ups a day. He introduces himself, pulls out his ID with a flip that is perhaps the only thing reminiscent of the agents on TV and, with a slight smile, says, "We have to get that out of the way."

The only thing this agent seems to notice is the wooden floor in my office. As he sits down, he leans over and brushes the floor with his hand. Before my department moved into the building, the floors were re-finished and polished and indeed they are worthy of his admiration. This gives me the opportunity to explain the story of the building, from being an infirmary to a dorm and now housing our department. He nods, clearly appreciative of the effort that went into creating the beauty of these shiny floors.

From his briefcase, he pulls out a notebook, opening it to the list of questions, and we proceed. He explains that this student is applying for a position as an Intelligence Analyst, which means she will be analyzing data and looking for patterns that could help the FBI catch terrorists. For a moment, my perspective shifts and I think what it would mean to have this responsibility, the heavy weight of its consequences. To do this, he explains, she needs to have a security clearance and so he has been given the task of investigating her.

His questions about the student's maturity, intelligence, and academic ability, I can answer easily. Others, such as whether there are signs of drug abuse, financial problems, or questionable loyalty to the United States, I can only answer, saying, "Not as far as I know." I'm a little uncertain about the purpose of the question regarding whether the student has had relations with foreign nationals. However, I'm pleased when he asks if there are any indications that she might have biases against a particular group of people. It's a good question. But he stumbles slightly with the wording, explaining "with people who are different" then hesitates and adds, "Well, no one is really different."

We digress only momentarily when one of the questions takes us to how the student body at my university has changed over time. He grew up in the area, he tells me, but he didn't have enough money to date a girl from this university. "If you wanted to go out with me," he says, "you had to be willing to ride the bus." I learn he went to a nearby college then joined the army. After that, I assume he acquired his position with the FBI. "It's a service to your country," he says at one point. There is a sincerity in his voice that makes me wish I could have more than a glimpse into this man's life.

When the questions are finished, I'm almost a little disappointed. I show him to the correct door to get to the lot where he has parked his car. Back at my desk, I can hear his footsteps outside my office as he goes down the stairs. I'm hoping he doesn't notice the camel in the window looking out at him.

To Walk Cautiously in the World

MONDAY MORNING, I wake up bleary eyed, pour my first cup of coffee, sit at the kitchen table, and unfold the day's newspaper. "Osama Bin Laden Dead" in all caps, large font, stares back at me. The headline is at the top of the page above the name of the paper. I blink—Is it April Fool's? No, it's already May. I repeat the headline as a question directed at my husband. "Yes," he answers, "It's been on the news all morning." I read, taking in the information—this man we have been trailing for ten years captured overnight. I turn the pages and stop at a short column. NATO has killed one of Gadhafi's sons and three grandchildren. How old were these children? Why were they killed? Is this really ok? But there is no more information. Most of the articles are about Bin Laden. On one of the inside pages, there is a picture of a crowd of people outside the White House celebrating, fists shooting in the air, their faces open in smiles, an American flag wrapped around one person, the white house a small brightly lit icon in the background. My husband tells me the celebratory crowds raised their hands and shouted "U.S.A." What does this mean? Is this our triumph as a nation?

My brain is waking up slowly as I pour the second cup of coffee. I'm not sure how I feel—I'm glad that Bin Laden is gone, that he can no longer hurt another person. His death makes me keenly aware of the tragedy of his life, the destruction that he has caused to others. But is it ever ok to celebrate a death? Something in all this unsettles me. My mind calls up the image of those who gathered to have picnics and watch lynchings.

Beneath the headline, there is a picture of Bin Laden on one side and a picture of Obama on the other. My husband points out the similarity—skin tone, features. My daughter says they have the same nose. I look back and forth at the photos. Yes, visually, they could be cousins. The trick of circumstance that creates us—our parents, the country of our birth, the religion we are born into, the range of choices we are allowed in living our lives. Pull one thread and we can unravel into a different life. We are not so distant from each other.

I fold the newspaper and put it in the recycling bin—my attempt to push the news aside, to remove it from my daily life. At the dinner table that evening, Celine tells us that one of her friends said she thought of her when she heard about Bin Laden. What does this mean? How does this man's life intersect with my daughter who is Egyptian/African American, born in the United States, and a fourteen-year-old middle school student? She goes on to tell us that her classmates were joking around, claiming they had killed Bin Laden. Something about all this disturbs us, yet none of us can quite pinpoint the source of our feelings. Yasmine says no one said much at her school, but she also explains that she had made a decision that morning to tune it all out. It's a protective shield that I know she has used before. Inappropriate remarks, ignorance expressed by others—she lets them slide past her, skimming across her surface to keep them from penetrating and harming her.

Just yesterday, our daughters were trying to convince us that racism today is not as bad as it was in the past, and the other was arguing that racism can be expressed by a variety of people. My husband, who is African American, and I gave them examples of the way that history seeps into the present, and the way we must remain on guard—that as a minority, you must develop that keen sense of awareness, be somewhat cautious in your interactions with others. No, they argued, it's not right to be suspicious of certain people, and everyone experiences discrimination. They believe that some things remain locked in the past, and the present we live in is a better place. We rallied back and forth—they find our views almost prejudiced and we find their perception of the world to be naïve. Yet, a part of me hopes they are right, that the world they grow into will indeed be relieved of its heavy past.

After dinner, I decide to walk to the grocery store to pick up a few things. It has been a warm day, and the evening breeze makes the walk pleasant. I'm enjoying this neighborhood where we have recently moved, a middle class area of mostly single family homes and also a number of apartment complexes. I see a young boy riding his bike, a woman dressed in a sari pushing a baby carriage, and two other women talking. There are so many newcomers to this country who start their lives in these kinds of apartments. My aunt and uncle lived in a similar place, the building occupied by immigrants from various countries, everyone complaining about the distinctive food smells seeping under their doorways. I'm wondering if these immigrants will eventually move out and buy homes in a more secluded suburb, if they will miss the community of these buildings. I approach the store and note a few young boys sitting on one of the tables outside. As I walk by, one of them yells out, "Osama Bin Laden." His body has turned in my direction and his voice is aimed toward me. I'm the only one walking past them. A hard rock in the pit of my stomach—fear even here in the open sidewalk where it's still daylight.

From the corner of my eye, I note how young the boy is, barely in middle school. I continue walking, my steps in the same beat carrying the hard edge inside me. My steadiness pushed by the need to survive, to protect myself.

Once inside the store, I look out to get a closer look at the boys, but they are already gone, perhaps running away from their own attempt at bravery. I linger, making my selections slowly. The truth is I feel slightly embarrassed at the way I've been shaken by the boy's shout. I call my husband to ask whether I should buy strawberries or raspberries even though I have already placed the raspberries in the cart. I call two more times, asking mundane questions. My husband's response grows irritated. I know the ring of the phone is disruptive. He might be reading, listening to music, or just following his thoughts. But right now, I'm grateful to simply be his annoying wife. The truth is I just want to hear the voice of someone who cares about me, who does not see my ethnicity every time he looks at me, the comfort of being perceived as a person in its purest term.

What did those boys see when I walked past them? Do I look like Bin Laden? Maybe it's the eyebrows—those thick, curved lines outlining our face and making us look suspicious. My physical appearance is elusive—I've been identified as Italian, Spanish, African American. The combination of my darker complexion, brown eyes, black hair, and sharp angled nose lends itself to multiple interpretations depending on the onlooker's gaze. Egyptian is not the first possibility that comes to most people's mind. But when an incident occurs that highlights Arabs in the media, people's assumptions shift, and I'm defined in relation to the day's news. We are chameleons transformed by the political events of our time. I'm reminded of the Sikh man murdered shortly after 9/11, presumed to be Arab at that moment in history. Was this the boys' attempt to imagine themselves as heroes? Shouting at me, labeling me the enemy—how far would their aggression go?

Entangled in the thread that connects all of us are also these young boys. We exist at the same time and in the same place—their shout only brought us closer. I wonder if I should have responded. I could have said, "Yes, he's my long lost cousin." But the sarcasm of my comment might have diffused before it reached them. Or maybe I should have sworn at them in Arabic, taken refuge in words whose meaning they cannot understand, scaring them with those guttural sounds, using their own fears against them. But that might have only escalated the situation instead of letting it sift back into dust.

The next morning, there is another short article about the attack on Gadhafi's compound. The grandchildren who were killed were one infant and two toddlers. They were too young to know what they had been born into, still unable to recognize their inheritance, or decide what to do with it. What sense does it make to destroy them? And to cause agony to those who loved and cared for them? The rest of the paper is filled with details of the attack that killed Bin Laden along with three men and one woman.

I'm not sure what we are left with at the end of all this. But I tell my children that after the day's events, I'm not quite ready to let my guard down. They nod in acknowledgement. And this is what we have—the politics that reach into our lives, the history that will not release itself from the present. I still hope for a future where my children do not have to build a protective shield, where they do not have to walk cautiously in the world.

The Last Camping Trip

PEOPLE IN EGYPT DON'T CAMP. No one owns a tent, a sleeping bag, or a camp stove. The notion of "roughing it" is nonexistent. Life offers enough challenges, from overthrowing the rule of the colonial British Empire to ousting a president after thirty years of a corrupt regime. In between, there have been bread riots, Israeli planes flying overhead, presidential assassinations, an earthquake, and the occasional sandstorm. In addition, the environment presents certain obstacles against the camping experience. There are no woods in Egypt. Pitching a tent in a fifty square foot grassy area surrounded by the honking of traffic and the possibility of a car taking a short cut over you holds little appeal even for the bravest. Of course there is the abundant desert and there are those who gravitate toward it out of habit, necessity, or a desire for the exotic, but for your typical Egyptian, the desert is simply a permanent presence along with the unmoving traffic and the pyramids.

Egyptians struggle daily to achieve the basics of life. With eighty million people and a population that increases by one million every nine months, apartments are a rare commodity. Couples wanting to get married not only have to spend years saving enough to meet the rapidly increasing prices, but they also have to use every connection they have, such as asking their third cousin twice removed to check with their great uncle who has a neighbor whose aunt works in the bank where the owner of the new apartment building has his accounts. By the time the couple have accumulated enough money and found someone who could actually rent them an apartment, they may have aged beyond the ability to bear children, which may not be a bad thing given the population growth. Employment opportunities remain equally elusive. Nasser's promise to provide a job in the civil service to every college graduate has now led to a waiting list longer than the Nile. These economic obstacles compounded by the shortage of housing create a maze of challenges for those youths attempting to build their adult life.

If they are fortunate enough to surmount these difficulties, a young couple will begin their life in their own apartment, usually procured by the husband. That apartment will be fully furnished, generally at the expense of the bride's family who has probably been accumulating the necessary items since their daughter's birth. It's not uncommon to enter a home and find a brand new washer and dryer in the corner of a dining room, camouflaged by a large tablecloth, or a bedroom that contains two sets of furniture, one pushed against the wall as if trying to remain unobtrusive. The financial sacrifices by the bride and groom as well as their families result in a couple truly grateful to be entering their own home. To leave all this in order to "get away from it all" when getting to all this has been the point provides little motivation for confronting the hazards of the outdoor landscape.

This inheritance of culture is perhaps the reason I've always been wary of the camping experience. Why leave everything you have worked so hard to earn in order to toss and turn all night on a rocky surface and to stumble through sticks and brambles when you need to use the bathroom? When I ask this question, I'm given answers such as "to connect with nature" and "to appreciate what you have." Let me assure you that I do appreciate what I have. After a long journey filled with counting coins, tutoring football players, and supporting the student loan industry to arrive at a place where I can enjoy the basic necessities of life, it is my firm belief that the world's greatest inventions are indoor plumbing and central air conditioning. And I do understand the value of connecting to nature. I'm happy to sit in a park and read a book or go on a hike as long as it doesn't include any upward inclines. However, at the end of this bonding with nature, I prefer to sleep between the coolness of my own sheets on a bed that kindly conforms to the indentations of my body.

Despite these beliefs, I have succumbed to the attempt to enlarge my cultural boundaries by camping. My daughters' school requires an annual camping trip. Up until second grade, they ask a parent to accompany each child. Yasmine was attached enough to her father that she was quite content to have him join her on these adventures meant to create bonding experiences and ensure that this innovative private school graduated children who had an appreciation for the natural world. This was all well and good, as long as I wasn't the accompanying parent. My husband, like so many good Americans, grew up camping with his family and often reminds us with pride that he was a loyal member of the Webelos and the Explorer Scouts. The problem began when it was Celine's turn to join these overnight outings. She was not quite as fond of her father. Her general response to his attempt at expressing parental affection was to either scream or bop him on the head. There was little room for negotiation. I was the chosen one for the camping trip.

After acquiring the basics of a waterproof tent and a sleeping bag guaranteed to keep me warm to twenty degrees, we also purchased a foam pad to create some barrier between me and the rocky earth, along with a super flashlight to guide us to the bathroom. That left the problem of coffee. My coffee maker at home is set up the night before with the correct amount of filtered water and cinnamon hazelnut coffee, guaranteeing that the brewing process will begin at 5:30am, so, once my eyes open, all I have to do is pour my cup. This hi-tech coffeemaker was a gift from my family one mother's day. It was given with love and the knowledge that speaking to me before my first cup of coffee was a dangerous endeavor. This coffeemaker is no mere appliance, but my guide to navigating the light of morning and surviving the travails of each day. I'm not the type who can suspend my caffeine addiction until everyone has gathered around the campfire and wait for the aluminum pot to bring water to a boil only to be offered a half cup of lukewarm pale brown liquid. My desire for coffee arouses me as my eyes blink open.

I googled to see if anyone had invented a battery-operated coffee maker. My search yielded nothing, although I did learn that the amount of battery power required to heat water was too great to make such an invention possible. My options were few, and I succumbed to taking a six-pack of Frappuccino. It didn't require refrigeration, would not attract bears, and would temporarily subdue my addiction.

All this would have been fine had I not forgotten to take it with me. After my husband dropped us off with all our paraphernalia, I realized the omission. The only option was to have him deliver the six-pack to our colleague, Renee, who was arriving later to accompany her son. This could have worked had Renee along with her husband and son not been the epitome of nature people. They live at the edge of the world, up a mountain and down a long winding dirt road. Their mailbox is five miles from their house. Our first introduction to their home was a faculty party to celebrate Renee's tenure. The invitation said to wear comfortable clothes, as there would be opportunities for hiking—already I was suspicious. It was our first semester at this small university in southwest Virginia where we had unexpectedly found ourselves. We drove and continued to drive, following the directions we were given. The asphalt streets gave way to dirt roads and then a rocky path that seemed intended only for foolish mules. There were no houses, no other cars, no indication that this portion of the world had been discovered by human beings. I suggested we surrender and turn back around—perhaps this was some kind of faculty orientation, a joke played on new professors to initiate them into the fold. My husband was far more optimistic and insisted we continue a bit more. He turned the wheel to meet the road's curves as the kids in the back moaned with each bump until we arrived at the promised mirage: an A-frame house nestled in the lap of a mountain as if it had grown out of the soil. I continue to fluctuate between admiration and disbelief at this lifestyle. True to character, Renee walked through the campsite, swinging my six pack of Frappuccino in hand, announcing the arrival of my addiction. I hung my head in shame and accepted the delivery.

The next morning I woke up early, unraveling myself from the twisted sleeping bag. I could only hear the quiet of the day, no rumblings from any of the other tents. I released the cap of one of my Frappucinos, and, with the first cold sip, the disjunction between nature and this overly sweet and artificially flavored drink entered my throat.

Our first activity of the day was a hike. Since these were five and six year olds, I naively assumed this would be an easy hike. As we made our way along the trail, it narrowed, requiring us to move single file, and began to slope up until I realized we were literally climbing a mountain. I tugged at my body to meet the demands of the climb, but the drop-off down the side only inches from my footsteps did little to encourage me. My confidence sunk as I placed one foot carefully in front of the other only to see Renee's five-year-old son race up the incline like a mountain goat. Even my own daughter was betraying me by steadily climbing with seemingly no effort. It had to be her father's American genes, I decided. My huffing and puffing along with my slow progress resulted in the offer of some help, and soon I was being pulled by the person ahead of me and pushed by the person behind me. It was an undignified ascent to say the least. At the top, we were commanded to appreciate the lovely view, by which point my self-esteem had rolled down the side of the mountain and fallen into a ravine.

When I decided to give camping another try—my memory of previous camping experiences having retreated to the recesses of my mind—I rented us a cabin in a state park. This, I thought, would be safe. After all, the cabin had cots, a bathroom, and air conditioning. The natural world would remain safely outside, and we could close the door on it. What I didn't anticipate was all the items we would need to pack in order to leave the comfort of our home and connect with nature: blankets and pillows; pots, pans, and dishes; shampoo, soap, and towels; and of course food. We needed three meals a day and snacks for a family of four plus the essentials: feta cheese and olive oil.

Hazy memories of childhood take me back to my paternal grandparents' house to open the large tin of feta cheese. I recall being told that the cheese had been placed in the large aluminum container and soldered shut, then buried for several months to achieve its full flavor. The opening of the tin was a family ritual: the large container emerged, and my grandfather unwrapped the gauze around it. Rust rimmed its edges, and whatever writing or color had once been on it had faded, as if the can had shed its skin under the earth. My grandfather tapped a knife around the edge until the top could be pried off and the contents released. Extended relatives gathered as squares of white cheese were cut and distributed among all of us. My tongue wrapped around the taste of the cheese whether I ate it as a sandwich with cucumbers or with watermelon on a warm summer evening. It was the tingling of salt and cream in my mouth. Now, years later, I packed my small tin of feta bought at the Arab grocery store along with olive oil and garlic, knowing that these items would improve our chances of survival in the wilderness.

The first day of our camping trip went well enough with some mild exploring and settling into our cabin. That evening, we sat outside and I made some hot chocolate. As the leaves rustled in the wind and the sun set, we seemed to have achieved a union with nature. The next morning, we sat by the lake while my husband, who had complained of a headache, slept. Later in the day, we decided to take a walk along one of the trails. A light breeze came through the trees, but the calm was abruptly interrupted when a giant bell hornet buzzed in circles above us. Emerging from the foliage, it seemed startled at finding itself in bright light and unable to regain its sense of direction. It buzzed like an alien creature grown beyond the proportions of its natural size—brownish in color with a coat of fur, it appeared intent on our destruction. The bearer of misfortune landed on Celine's head and zoomed away, leaving a sharp sting that resulted in her jumping up and down in agony. We ran haphazardly back to the cabin where we attempted to soothe her.

I called the rangers for help and they arrived with a potion to put on my daughter's head. This relieved the pain but did little to alleviate the trauma. Celine recounted the tale of the bee's attack on constant replay as her older sister vowed destruction to all bees in the land and ventured outdoors with her weapons of rocks and sticks. She proceeded to chase each bee in the vicinity, actually succeeding in causing the demise of several. By this point, my husband's headache had achieved full-blown maturity, causing him to remain in a horizontal position. His occasional attempts to rise only resulted in having the cabin spin him around in circles, forcing him back on the cot. As I drifted to sleep, listening to the moaning of my family, my brain recalled the headache my husband had had a week earlier after eating Yasmine's chocolate birthday cake, and my last thought before sleep was the awareness that he was allergic to chocolate.

This was not quite the family nature vacation I had envisioned. We packed up the next morning, my husband nursing the residue of his headache, Celine rubbing her head with phantom pains of the sting, and Yasmine still plotting revenge on all bees. I packed up my feta cheese and olive oil, along with the lessons I had acquired—nature and humans were not meant to interact too closely, and the next time we went on vacation, there would be no attempt to commune with nature. A five star hotel in an urban oasis among concrete and skyscrapers would do nicely.

Walking Home

TWICE A WEEK, I take the three mile walk home after teaching—from downtown through neighborhoods, past vacant lots, unkempt yards, and front porches with no railings to enclose them, their borders edging into the street.

Houses stretch along this main avenue, staring into the pavement of road with cars passing in transit. The neighborhood is punctuated by clothing and gestures—a woman sweeps a porch, a woman wears a sari—where refugees approach the city, a new life begging entrance into this world. And my own history tucked inside my pocket—a small studio apartment shared between my parents and an aunt and uncle for six months, sleeping on a bed that opens in the evening, laid out in the kitchen where I'm bound into covers by an aunt whose laughter echoes against tight walls.

My steps continue, leaning into the incline of uphill sidewalk. A dog wanders a front yard with a sign that says to keep off the grass; I learn to look for him on my way home, his loneliness cornered against the fence. No brightly formulated green lawns here, the edge of grass meeting concrete blending the view from house to street.

Only the black men I pass acknowledge me. One man offers a barely perceptible nod; another gives me a clear good morning, his gaze direct; one waves from his seat on a front porch. I nod, respond, wave back.

Years of walking inside city streets, my appearance elusive to each gazer, I've learned the etiquette of acknowledgment. Return the greeting of black men—it's only recognition of our mutual existence that is requested/ keep my eyes low when passing white men—better my look not be misconstrued for an invitation/ keep an even pace against the Spanish coming from other men—no way to explain it's a case of mistaken identity. Always keep a steady beat of movement.

I'm a short dark woman with an ethnic appearance not easily identified, but it's enough to exclude white. The dark color of my skin is the luggage I carry with me. It marks my steps through these sidewalks that take me home.

Nothing to guide me but air-wind-breath—I inhale each city, learn to move in this new world, firmly grounding myself in constant motion.

The 10th Anniversary

THE 10TH ANNIVERSARY OF 9/11 arrives with constant reminders that it's approaching—it's on the news, it's in the papers, it's in the air—conversations rise and fall around it and our memory retrieves that day. Where we were, what we felt. For those who lost loved ones, for those who were in New York, I cannot imagine the experience. Our anticipation of the day is marked by those reminders and those memories. There will be events to commemorate the day and to remember those who died and those who helped others. We await the day, sensing its arrival and re-living our experience of it.

I'm wary of this approaching anniversary; I keep trying to sidestep the constant recollection of it. Like previous anniversaries of 9/11, I plan to stay at home that day—no one in my family is allowed to make plans, to leave what I hope can be the safety of our home. And this year, with Yasmine in her first year of college, I send her a message, reminding her "Be careful—Sunday is the 10th anniversary of 9/11. Stay close to campus." "Don't worry," she responds. "I know. I'm planning on just staying in and doing homework." Even though she was only eight when those events took place,the years following have taught her their significance and the potential of danger. Many of us who are Arab American stay close to home on this day, fearful that the anger following 9/11 could erupt again, uncertain of how someone might react, how their anger might unleash. Our own safety is nothing we can take for granted.

I struggle to understand my own response this year. Why do I want to avoid this upcoming commemoration? Listening to an NPR segment, recounting stories of what people were doing on September 10 and how the next day impacted their lives, I'm deeply moved by what I hear. But there are other stories that remain in silence. No one is talking about how this day changed the lives of Arab Americans. No one is talking about those who were assaulted, harassed, and murdered because overnight they had become the image of the enemy. No one talks about the anger that translated into violence against innocent people. Nothing about how that sense of fear became our greatest enemy as people turned against each other. The Sikh man murdered in Mesa, Arizona because he was presumed to be Arab. The grocery store owned by a Palestinian in Clifton, New Jersey where someone wrote "Leave this Country" on the window and tore the American flag hung outside the store. The Muslim woman in San Gabriel, California who was attacked while grocery shopping, beaten by another woman who yelled at her "America is only for white people." The way an entire segment of our population was re-imagined as terrorists. And the government officials who advocated having Muslims and Arab Americans carry special IDs and suggested building internment camps for Arab Americans and anyone perceived to be an enemy, including those who are citizens.

I open my local newspaper on Sunday morning, knowing it will be filled with articles relating to 9/11, and I hold onto a small bit of hope that there will be something in there about how 9/11 impacted the lives of Arab Americans. I flip the pages, read the re-telling of that day's events, the recollections of those who remember, the experiences of those who were there. There is nothing. Not one reference to how Arabs were affected by this event; not one Arab American voice in the paper. I feel silenced by this commemoration. Within these memories of the event, within this writing of history, the experience of Arab Americans has been erased from the history of that day.

Celine is learning about the cold war in school—she watches Dr. Seuss's The Butter Battle with new eyes and says, "People sure don't learn much from history." But to learn from history, we must first know it. How we remember 9/11 and teach its history will determine what we learn. Every time I teach a book relating to the Armenian genocide or the Japanese internment camps, I ask my students how many of them have learned about these events in school, and at most one or two raise their hands. The story of Arab Americans and 9/11 has been buried beneath the surface; it has become another silence in our history.

What I remember is the phone call from my husband telling me to turn on the news, watching those horrific images in disbelief, the violence too unreal to take in, and another fear rising in me, the fear of what would happen if whoever did this was Arab—how this would affect all of us as a nation. This dual fear of the violence I was watching and the potential of further violence remains with me. If we are to remember 9/11, we cannot erase the parts we don't like—we must remember all the stories that mark this event in our history.

The Package

MID-SEPTEMBER: returning home from a long day of teaching, office hours, and the hum of university life. Dinner needs to be cooked, the cat needs to be fed, and papers need to be graded. My eye catches the flashing of the answering machine as I enter, balancing my heavy bag while dodging the cat so he doesn't escape. When I press the button on the machine, I expect it will be another message for the mysterious Jerry C. We've been in this house for over a year, but the calls persist. One debt collector after the next is searching for this man who is clearly in a lot of trouble. At first, we tried to ignore the calls, and then we answered in hopes of putting a stop to them by explaining that this was no longer Jerry C's number, that the caller had hit a dead end. But these were automated calls; only on rare occasions did we succeed in pressing enough keys to reach a human voice. Jerry C became the invisible member of our household, an elusive presence whom we learned to accept. This time when I press the button, I hear a befuddled human voice, someone calling from our local post office, saying something about a package that is damaged, that smells like Apple Jack and needs to be picked up.

My husband informs me that Apple Jack is some kind of alcohol, and I imagine the smell of fermented sour apples seeping through cardboard like a menacing warning. I rummage through the possibilities, combining the information from the message with the fact that it's September, and there is only one conclusion. It's 4:30 and the post office closes at 5:00, but I know this can't wait. My husband and I jump in the car for the quick two-minute ride.

It's a small post office that serves our neighborhood. There is an assortment of boxes, envelopes, and other mailing supplies for sale and a counter where usually two people are working. When it's my turn, I go up and ask for the person who called me. He's summoned from the back, and when he approaches me, I state my name and reiterate his phone message.

He raises an eyebrow, says nothing, and goes to the back of the post office. When he re-emerges with the box, I'm relieved to see that it has been placed in a plastic bag. This keeps the tiny fruit flies circling around it from looking too obvious. The man repeats his suspicion of the Apple Jack smell. Then he casually mentions that after the arrival of the package, he spent the day googling my name. It's a bit disconcerting to realize that I have been under such scrutiny. I wonder what this man discovered as he spent his day browsing the virtual world—perhaps my position as a professor assured him of my innocence, then again my publications as an Arab American writer might have sent out a warning flag. Did he suspect that someone was shipping me the makings of a bomb?

I want to prove my innocence, so I open the box to discover what I suspected—there are fresh yellow dates, still on the vine, some crisp and others with brown patches, showing the beginning of over-ripening. There is a Middle Eastern grocery store in Boston that carries those dates in September when they're in season. Each fall, I remember these dates and hope for their arrival. If my parents manage to make the trip to the store, then my antic-ipated package arrives. When I open the box in my kitchen, it releases the smell of palm trees with heavy bunches of dates hanging from the top of the trunk camouflaged by green leaves. However, the alcohol smell emanating from this box is not the fault of the dates; the box also holds mangos that have squashed and leaked in the process of being transported. This explains the Apple Jack smell and the fruit flies that precipitated such suspicion.

To prove the innocence of this package, I pluck a perfect yellow date off the vine and offer it to this man who has spent his day researching me. His hand approaches the date with caution, but he takes it and attempts a small bite. I know from his expression that he can taste the crisp texture of the date that yields to a hard sweetness. Hopeful, I attempt to give him a few more, but he kindly declines, saying, "This is my little bit of knowledge for the day." I don't insist, knowing he has taken enough steps into a foreign world. At least I have removed the stain of guilt from my reputation.

When I call my mother to thank her and explain the condition of the package upon its arrival, she justifies herself, saying that after she put the dates in the box, there was room left. My mother's boxes arrive stuffed to the brim, and at the bottom of Christmas or Easter presents, we're likely to find a bag of crushed sesame cookies bought at the church sale or a half-full box of chocolates or a sandwich bag of assorted candies. This time she looked around to see what she could add, and her eye settled on the mangos. Instead of explaining that mangos have made their way as far as the supermarkets of our small city in southwestern Virginia, I offer a simple thank you.

My next task is to pluck some of the best dates and create a new box, this one to send to my daughter, Yasmine, who is in college. She is my companion in the love of this fruit that is still a rare find in America. I select the ones that remain yellow and sharp and carefully prepare the package, placing the dates in green plastic bags intended to keep fruit fresh for a longer period of time. The next day after mailing them, I send her a message, warning her of the package, while keeping its contents a surprise, but I stress the imperative need to pick it up as soon as it arrives. I want to avoid any possibility that she might acquire a reputation for receiving suspicious mail at her university. The next day when I check Facebook, I know that the dates have once again found their destination, as her status reads: "I'm eating home in the form of fresh dates."

TIME DIFFERENCE

The Egyptian Uprising
January 25 - February 11
2011

January 2010

WHEN WE STEP OUT OF THE LUXOR AIRPORT, a taxi driver wearing a brown *galabeya* catches our attention immediately. Several drivers are standing in a makeshift line, taking turns for the customers. "One hundred pounds," he says, to take us from the airport to our cruise boat. I'm not sure of the distance, but I know this is a tourist price, although perhaps a bit less since he assumes we are all Egyptian. I can't call up the effort to negotiate, and I agree.

As the taxi enters the streets of Luxor, we all breathe in the quiet air of this small city. There is little traffic and the taxi moves smoothly. I make a comment to the driver about how much nicer this is than Cairo, where the traffic holds you still on every street, and a fifteen minute ride can easily take an hour or longer. We have grown frustrated with our limited movement, often opting to walk to our destination or minimizing the number of places we want to go. The city's congestion has multiplied since our last trip eight years ago, and now the sheer effort of movement from one location to another appears to require all reserves of energy. Each time we step into a taxi on Kasr el Aini Street, the main thoroughfare near our rented Garden City apartment, our feeling of success at catching a cab is quickly deflated by finding ourselves standing still in an endless line of traffic. Now, in the clear streets of Luxor, we relax from the tension that has built up in us.

The driver and I begin to talk. His English is almost fluent, and I learn that his brother travels to Chicago on a regular basis, selling papyrus at world fairs.

"Life here is hard, it is a torture, not just in Cairo, here too," he tells me. When I explain that my parents emigrated in 1969, he responds, "That was the best decision they made." There is a firm certainty to his voice.

We pursue our conversation, discussing where the frustration of life in Egypt might lead.

"It feels as if something will explode," I say.

I have felt the pent up tension of Cairo in a way that is different from any other time I have been in the city. We lived there for three years in the early 1990s, when the first Gulf war began. Bombs were going off, often targeting tourist sites and tour buses; bags left unattended were always suspicious. Our second trip for six months came right after 9/11 with a deepening anger spreading in the world. But I have never felt scared in Egypt. Not until this trip in January 2010, when I begin to fear that the country will erupt. I'm hoping we will leave before anything happens.

My Luxor taxi driver agrees, "Yes, and Egyptians are a passionate people. When it explodes, it will be something big."

Our cruise boat has a small number of passengers: there is the quiet Australian couple with two children; the Belgian couple with the wife who talks about her travels to anyone nonstop and whose poor husband looks like he's considering a leap into the Nile; the brother who has been living in Egypt for seven years and working for a petroleum company accompanied by his sister visiting from the States; the Scottish couple with the husband constantly trying to play tricks on the rest of us, pointing out an "alligator" in the Nile; the Egyptian family traveling with two young sons and a grandmother who constantly shouts "Ahmed" to call the younger boy; and the Egyptian newly-weds who miss several of the tourist excursions. We are an odd assortment travelling on this particular cruise boat among the hundreds of other boats that circle between Luxor and Aswan, making their living from tourists eager to see the monuments of ancient Egypt.

At each meal, the waiters greet us with smiles. They entertain our daughters, doing a magic trick by making salt water move to the edge of a plate with the touch of a finger. Their kindness is genuine, but it also comes with the expectation that we will respond with a generous tip. They are part of the middle class in Egypt, struggling to make a living. Several of them have gone to college, but faced with limited possibilities, they found that working as waiters on this boat offers more benefits, even though it means being away from their families for extended periods of time.

We enjoy our Nile cruise and the rest of our trip, fully aware that our ability to go where we want and buy what we please is the result of an exchange rate where each dollar is worth five Egyptian pounds, making us far wealthier than most Egyptians. It's an uneasy balance for us, taking pleasure in our unexpected wealth while being keenly aware of how high the prices have risen and the difficulty of making ends meet for most Egyptians.

January 2011

I don't think the taxi driver or I realized we were making a prediction, but the eruption we had anticipated comes one year later on January 25. This protest does not rise out of anger but out of the frustration and despair of living without any hope for the future. It comes from men who work two or more jobs and still cannot make enough to support their families; it comes from young people who have studied hard, gone to university to earn their degrees, and still cannot find jobs; it comes from women who can no longer feed their children when a kilo of cheese costs fifty pounds. And it comes from the traffic that does not move—leaving people at a standstill in their lives. The city has grown to a point where everyone has become paralyzed—no progress can be made, not as a nation and not as an individual. Egypt holds eighty million people in the palm of its hand, and the weight of their existence is more than the land can sustain.

When my parents were growing up in the 1950s, there were perhaps twenty million people in Egypt; when Mubarak took power in 1981, there were forty million people. Now there are over eighty million people in the country, eighteen million of whom live in Cairo. Providing enough resources for that many people creates serious problems. And each year the population increases by more than one million. Birth control is not easily available, lack of education and a fifty percent literacy rate limit people's awareness of their options, and the desire for a son can motivate the decision to have another child. The man who gave me a donkey ride at the Saqqara pyramids last January told me he has nine daughters. Eight were already married with their own children. The youngest was ten years old and her name was Dunia, which means the world. He told me with pride that he was able to educate all of them up to the middle school level. Nine children to clothes and feed and educate while he made his living giving donkey rides to the few tourists who opted for a donkey instead of the majestic camels or the familiar horses.

Even the best educated often end up driving taxis or selling cigarettes and candy in a kiosk. They are unable to make enough money to get an apartment so they can get married. The possibility of a future remains inaccessible. The cost of living keeps rising, making it hard for most people to meet their basic needs. Egypt's upper class continue to do well, but the middle class feel their lives becoming more restricted. While fifty pounds for a kilo of cheese is equivalent to ten dollars for us, it is a great deal of money for most Egyptians who make only a few hundred pounds a month. Each day becomes a struggle to make a living. This uprising emerges from a deep desire to live in a country where people can build a good life. As my aunt tells me, "Egyptians are not a greedy people. They just want what is enough to meet their needs."

The Protests

As soon as the protests begin, I call my family in Egypt. All of them are staying at home, hoping that things will calm down soon. The emails and phone calls tumble into my house almost simultaneously with friends and colleagues asking about my family. I have grown accustomed to Americans remaining distant from what's happening in other places, so this catches me by surprise. I have become a link, connecting them to the images entering their home through the TV screen.

I watch the protests on CNN and then switch to Al Jazeera in English online. I'm frustrated by the disruption of the news on TV with continuous commercials for losing weight and the endless reruns of sitcoms I find when I flip channels. Al Jazeera's coverage is continuous, and I am pulled into the streets rising up in Cairo. These are all familiar places. Tahrir Square is in the middle of the city. Its name was changed from Ismailia Square to Tahrir Square—meaning Liberation Square—by Gamal Abdel Nasser after the 1952 revolution, which finally gave Egypt its independence from Britain. On one side is the old American University in Cairo campus where my husband and I taught for three years. Since then, the university has built a larger campus on the outskirts of the city in a development called New Cairo. Perhaps it is far enough to be safe from the ensuing danger. But the old campus in the middle of Tahrir Square still houses continuing education and numerous university offices. For three years, our lives centered on this campus, teaching students whose world balanced East and West. The university was established in 1919, and its main building is a converted palace originally built in the 1860s for the Minister of Education, Khairy Pasha. Once you step through the gates, you enter an oasis in the middle of the urban landscape of Cairo. Here, there are trees, green sculpted gardens, flowers, and the wandering birds and stray cats fortunate to have found their way into this utopia. The Egyptian Museum, built in 1902, borders another edge of Tahrir. It's filled with the ancient relics that epitomize the grandeur of Egyptian history and attracts enough tourists to sustain the country's economy. At the other end is the Nile Hilton Hotel, built in 1959, one of the best hotels in the country, overlooking the Nile River. On the further end of the square sits the fifteen-story Mogamma building, built in 1951. Bureaucracy reigns through the halls of this gray architectural hulk where Egyptian citizens have to go to get ID cards, renew licenses, and procure any paperwork necessary to carry on their lives. Tahrir Square is the center of the city, its beating heart, and it is where the protesters converge.

Once the protests begin, I know they will not end quickly. Egyptians are hardheaded and stubborn. We pursue what we want even if everything indicates that we are bound for failure. And our stamina is infinite. As I watch these protests, I know that the people who have flooded these streets will not return home without achieving their goal. At one point, I catch a glimpse of an interview with a young protestor who says, "We have a PhD in stubbornness, and we have two PhDs in staying in Tahrir." But on the other side of the battle is Mubarak, equally stubborn. He is proud and wants to protect his reputation and legacy. This battle may outlast the attention span of most Americans.

I'm astounded by the clear voices of the protesters asking for Mubarak to leave, demanding a change from a corrupt government. I grew up under President Gamal Abdel Nasser. One of my earliest memories is sitting around the living room, listening to adults talk about politics. After the conversations ended, I was given clear, sharp warnings from my parents not to repeat anything I had heard outside the house. "Otherwise," my parents said, "they will make you disappear." There was no further explanation, and at the age of eight, my imagination wrapped in fear around the notion of disappearing. The idea that I would cease to exist frightened me to the core. I kept my mouth closed, learning that the utterance of words alone could harm you. That warning has stayed with me, and even as an adult, I am reluctant to speak about politics. Some fears remain embedded in you.

Egypt is not a country that advocates freedom of speech, but these protestors on the street have broken through these barriers, and there are too many of them for the government to make them disappear. They push up against the police, their bodies a force of will that makes these officers stumble backwards. On Al Jazeera, we hear my cousin, Timothy Kaldas, being interviewed. He was born and raised in the United States but went to Egypt three years ago to study Arabic and stayed, becoming one of the top wedding photographers in the country. Now his camera has turned in a different direction, and he is documenting this uprising. His academic studies focusing on the Middle East have led him to this place at this moment of history, and there is nothing to barricade him from the politics that have come to life outside of his Zamalek apartment. His mother wanted him to leave the country—catch any plane at any cost. But he resisted, choosing to remain in the midst of this uprising, his camera leading him toward the streets. The interviewer asks him, "What has struck you the most in the last day or so, something you've seen that you could not have imagined seeing in Egypt?" And he answers, "The thing that struck me perhaps the most…just watching the complete shedding of the political apathy that so many of us have observed or thought we were observing in Cairo and Egypt for so long….There's always the sense that I'm powerless as an individual. That sense is gone."

The persistence of these protesters was partly motivated by the fact that Mubarak had been president for the last thirty years. During previous elections, people were given the choice of voting for Mubarak or not voting for Mubarak. This has been Egypt's version of democracy. The few candidates who were allowed to be on the ballot for the last election had no chance of winning. When we were in Egypt a year ago, I heard a great deal about how Mubarak has been preparing his son, Gamal Mubarak, to take over the presidency. The assumption that his son would be the next president angered many people because they felt that he was being forced on them, and once again they would be denied the right to choose their own leader.

For those in their thirties and younger, Mubarak is the only president they have known. This may help to explain their urgent desire to see a change in their government. Those who are older, like my aunt who is eighty, have lived a different history. My aunt was born when King Fuad was in power; she was a young woman when his son, King Farouk, was in control; she witnessed the 1952 revolution that overthrew the king and sent him into exile; and she has since lived under the presidency of Gamal Abdel Nasser, Anwar El Sadat, and Hosni Mubarak.

Many of the people participating in these protests are middle class. They are educated and skilled at using the internet, which has been instrumental in bringing so many people into the streets. There is a sense of pride among most Egyptians—this is the youth of Egypt. Even those who remain at home are able to hold their heads higher at the courage exhibited by those carrying out the protests, finally doing what no one thought could be done. There is a sense of cooperation—people working together to make sure that food, water, and medical care is provided, and that the protests remain peaceful. We are all struck by the ordinary citizens who link their arms to surround the Egyptian Museum and protect their heritage from looters.

By the fifth day, violence has taken over and the looting and burning is in full force. Something has shifted, and the government's lack of response has turned frustration into anger. This destruction occurs between the time the police are pulled off the streets and before the military is brought out. All the police stations are destroyed. I call my aunt again. She is eighty and lives alone. The tenants in her building are all Christian, and there is the ongoing fear of not knowing which way these protests will turn. They could move against the minority of Christians in the country. My aunt is more distraught with each phone call: they have robbed and vandalized the bank on the corner of her street—these protests are outside her door. She lives in Giza in the middle of the city. They are stealing from restaurants, from jewelry shops, she tells me. "It's terrible," I respond. "Yes," she says, "They are hungry. Do you know what it means that they are hungry?" My aunt is middle class, keenly aware of the rising prices that affect her daily life. "The prices have gone up," she says, "I used to spend a hundred pounds to feed myself. Now, three hundred barely buys me anything."

When my mother called my uncle on the first day of the protests, my uncle, who is well off, said to her, "It's nothing, just a few young people on the street, nothing to worry about." Perhaps the rich stay in denial the longest, unwilling to imagine that their lives could change, secure in what they have acquired and believing it gives them a stability that makes them immune. Now my uncle tells me, "The streets are destroyed. They looted and burned the duty free shop behind our house…thank goodness the wind didn't blow the flames toward us." My uncle lives in Mohandessein, right near one of the main shopping districts—all those shops looted; everything is destruction.

"What about Old Cairo?" I ask my aunt. "Has it gone that far?" I'm concerned about my father's family—another aunt lives there with her son who is bed-ridden and her other son usually checks on her daily. "No, there is nothing much there," she tells me. "It's a poor area; there is nothing for them to take."

I hang up and call my aunt in Old Cairo. Her voice is the same— "Everything is fine," she says, "Things are still open, but the line to get bread is too long, so some days we don't get bread and people are charging more. The tomatoes used to be one and a half pounds a kilo; now they're asking three pounds. But my son comes every day; the trains are still running. How are you and how are the kids?" she asks. "It's so nice of you to call." She is watching the news, but her life has sustained its routine during this uprising. She persists in her daily rituals, seemingly immune to these political changes. They had little yesterday and they will have little tomorrow regardless of who rules the country.

The protests have extended their reach to the suburbs of Maadi and Heliopolis where others in my family live. A recreation club in Maadi is burned down. I'm remembering the City Stars Mall in Heliopolis, seven stories tall with over 600 stores. There is H&M, US Polo, Adidas, as well as familiar restaurants—Fuddruckers, Ruby Tuesday, Starbucks. I wonder if that mall has also fallen prey to the looting.

Even when things begin to calm down, this damage with the destruction of buildings, the looting, and the complete loss of tourism will take a long time to fix. Everyone will feel the effect, especially tour guides, taxi drivers, those who work in hotels and restaurants and those selling a variety of goods from Pharaonic statues to spices, depending almost entirely on tourists to make their living. I'm thinking of the men who rowed out on their small boats in Aswan, coming dangerously close to our cruise boat. They enticed us by placing their various souvenirs in plastic bags and throwing them up to us in the hopes that we would buy them and throw the money down to them. It's a difficult way to make a living. But now I imagine there are hardly any cruise boats on the Nile that can allow these men to make a few pounds.

I call my aunt again. She tells me many of the stores, especially in the center of the city, have closed, but last Sunday, the bakeries were open and people could buy bread. Today, she was able to buy some cheese. She says, "I have plenty of bread, some cheese, lots of tea, and sugar. I am fine."

In the United States

I go through my own routine here, taking care of my family and going to work. But I'm pulled by the images on the screen into Egypt's streets. My ability to go to the grocery store in this place of free movement is unsettled by my knowledge that each of my family members in Egypt has only so much food in their house. How they will survive is not certain. My existence in this country of abundance and stability seems only an illusion. My kids have to ask me everything twice. I'm barely able to listen, to remember that I am here.

The seven hour time difference between Egypt and the US has disintegrated. I get up at six am and call my aunt—for her, it's one in the afternoon. My cousin's mother in the U.S. stays up until midnight so she can call her son in Zamalek at seven am, hoping he has not yet gone out into the streets with his camera. The mobiles have been disconnected; the internet has been shut off. Our phone calls collapse time and distance, and we exist in the same moment speaking through these land lines, the only thing still holding us together. We have returned to those first years after immigration when we would dial anxiously, hoping that the connection would work, that we would reach the one we loved, that our computing of the time difference was correct, that the person was home. The online Al Jazeera in English streams into my house all day. My sense of time shifts to Egypt, and I have to remember to look at the clock, so I can calculate when I need to cook dinner, when my children need to get to school.

After the looting and the release of prisoners, people's fear has risen, and there are stories of thieves breaking into apartments. When I call my family, I learn that each apartment building has gathered its young men, and they have gone into the streets, taking whatever weapons they have—knives, guns, sticks. They are keeping watch every night to make sure that the tenants in each building are safe. They check people's IDs, and if anyone tries to harm someone, they turn them over to the military. My aunt tells me, "This is the first night I've been able to sleep—knowing those young men are out there protecting us."

I watch the transformation of Tahrir Square—where I taught for three years at the American University in Cairo, where I took visitors to see the antiquities at the Egyptian Museum, where I made a brave but futile attempt to get my Egyptian ID card through the bureaucracy of the Mogamma building, and where I strolled through the shops at the Nile Hilton. Now the square is brimming with people raising their voices and arms, carrying their handwritten signs in protest against a government that has lasted too long, a government threatening to turn into a monarchy. These voices in Tahrir create the momentum for moving the country forward, even though the future is unknown and no one has a clear plan, only a desire to regain the sense of hope that has disappeared. This is an uprising of frustration, of desire, a resistance against standing still—a will of people to feel alive and moving again.

Egyptians, no matter the struggle and the difficulty of their lives, were always ready to smile, to offer a kindness to someone else—it's called *henya* in Arabic—a gentleness of the soul—or el *aatafa*—a feeling of compassion and sympathy with another person. They have always been able to retain a feeling of joy at living. This is what has been lost with the lack of jobs, housing, and enough money to live at just the most basic level. No matter how much education, the jobs are too few, the salaries too low, and the prices too high. People can't find apartments, can't get married, can't move their lives forward, and everyone appears stranded in the midst of the Cairo traffic. The frustration and despair have risen over years; they have reached the point of eruption and must spill over into these streets.

For many Egyptians in America, distance has collapsed, and we find that we are pulled into the streets where people's voices are rising, that we are no longer standing in the natural serenity of a community park or the abundance of a supermarket or moving steadily along the highway to our destination. Even when the news is not on, I can hear the voices chanting, calling out, and they are a constant reverberation in my ears—we exist simultaneously in the flux of time and space.

The news tells us that there are two million people in Tahrir Square. The cameras from CNN, Al Jazeera, and BBC are focused on them, their perspective looking down. I imagine these camera men on the balcony or roof top of one of the buildings surrounding the square, having secured themselves a safe spot with a good view to bring us this image of the crowd surging in Tahrir. But as I watch the images, my eyes lose their focus, and I leave this crowd to walk down the streets that pull away from the square and move toward the neighborhoods I know. If there are two million people protesting in Tahrir then there are sixteen million people sitting in their homes in Cairo. This is where the news cameras cannot enter. This is the experience of the protests for most Egyptians—they are held captive in their homes, watching the news, and each day family members call each other to make sure others are okay and to exchange news that exists neither on our Western TV nor on the Egyptian state channel. In the morning, someone in each household is sent out to see if any stores are open, to buy what food is available, and to stand in the long lines in hopes of buying some bread. They make do with what they have. They are eager for this uprising to end, so they can return to their jobs and their children can go back to school. Their anxiety comes from not knowing what will happen next and how all of this will get resolved.

The waiting, the uncertainty, and the fear have dominated the experience of these protests for the majority of the population. There is not much for them to do besides listen to the news, call each other, and wait to see what comes next. They open their cupboards to look at what they have left. As long as the young men are standing outside each night guarding the buildings, there is some sense of safety, but how long can they keep watch? My aunt says, "We are managing fine, but I have no appetite. I go in the kitchen and eat what I find. We want to feel safe again, not scared. We want to go back out and walk in the streets. What is the good of having plenty of food if you don't feel safe? We need safety."

Each day, the hopeful announcement that the protests are ending and people are leaving Tahrir reveals itself to be only a rumor, and another day will be spent inside apartments, waiting and sharing news. Rumors begin to circulate: The government is paying people to stay in Tahrir and wreak havoc. The protestors have gone home. The only people in Tahrir are from Hamas, the Muslim Brotherhood, and Iran.

As the protests continue, people begin to step out of their homes, trying to move their lives forward again, to return to some sense of normalcy. Some of the banks and stores begin to open. The ATM machines are fixed and people can access their money. But the schools and universities remain closed. People are going out, but everything is moving slowly. It takes my cousin two and a half hours to get from her house in Maadi to my aunt's house in Giza, a trip that normally takes no more than a half hour.

In the midst of this turmoil, a friend emails my husband a series of photos from the protests—they are of "helmets." While the police wear bulletproof vests, some of the protestors have combined the materials available to them with some creativity to design a new line of protective gear. The first picture displays a man with three empty plastic soda bottles wrapped around his head, one on top and one on each side. Another photo shows a man balancing a cement brick on his head wrapped tightly with a cloth around his chin, another man is happily gesturing with an aluminum pot protecting his head. But the pièce de résistance of these captured shots is the man who has camouflaged his head with loaves of bread. With three loaves secured by masking tape, he raises both arms in the air with an expression of heroic invincibility. These images once again provide proof of Egyptian resourcefulness and resilience even in times of trouble.

Some of my favorite photos are taken by my cousin, Timothy Kaldas, whose camera has captured a few of the individual faces among the millions of protestors. There is the young boy riding on his father's shoulders, yelling into a megaphone while his father's face opens into a joyous smile. And there is the tiny girl, held by her mother, with the words "No to Mubarak" written on her forehead. Another photo shows two men sitting on the sidewalk, leaning against the side of a building. Both are asleep, one man's head resting on the shoulder of the other. Their slumber appears full and heavy, satiating their appetite for sleep. Perhaps they know each other or maybe they only found each other at this same spot, tired from the ongoing political struggle. Even in the midst of a revolution, a little rest is necessary.

Egyptian-American

WHEN THE PROTESTS IN EGYPT begin in January 2011, I receive numerous emails and phone calls asking about the events taking place. I'm part of a small community and I'm the only Egyptian in that community. I understand that I've become a kind of connection, a rope that stretches across the ocean for people, linking them to the distant news they're watching on their TV screen. I respond with emails and updates, sharing what I know from family members in Egypt. I accept this role—it's an extension of being the translator of language, of culture. It's a role that every child immigrant plays. But I also sense that my own identity is shifting with these political movements that are riding the waves across the ocean.

As the protests continue, the news cameras turn toward Egyptians in the U.S.—gatherings are being held in support of the uprising outside the Egyptian Embassies in New York and Washington D.C. For the first time, I hear the term Egyptian American being used. When I was growing up in the United States in the 1970s and 1980s, I struggled with how to name myself in this country that defines people by set terms. Despite the fact that Egypt is firmly located on the continent of Africa, I knew I wasn't African American, not in the way that it was understood. Labels, I quickly learned, were not literal definitions of identity but a conglomerate of history, politics, and perception all at constant play with one another. Despite learning that people from the Middle East and North Africa were officially categorized as white, I knew that this was also not true. My physical appearance, my cultural habits, and people's questions about camels and pyramids made it clear that I could not claim a white identity. The most accurate term to describe myself was Egyptian American, but when I used it, I was met with a puzzled look—this was not part of the vocabulary of identity in America.

At times I felt invisible—since I couldn't be defined, I was ignored. At other times, I felt like a primitive oddity—the stereotypes made me think that I should arrive turbaned and riding a camel. I learned to adapt, usually preferring to keep myself hidden. In high school, one of my friends announced that she had figured out what I was—"You're green," she said, with pride at her discovery. She had read that Arabs have olive complexions and had translated that information to a specific color that could define me. I humored her and took on my new green identity. In college, someone asked if I was black or white. I looked at the color of my skin and responded "Brown." But there was no such category, and my inquisitor brushed aside my attempt at placing myself in the gradations of the color wheel.

Attending graduate school in the Midwest in the 1980s, I discovered that I had become exotic and sexualized in ways that once again made me prefer to retreat into invisibility. Those of us who did not exist firmly in the categories of black and white, but in that liminal space between the two had suddenly become more interesting to other people. I adopted the term Arab American, choosing the comfort of being part of a larger group. At least in the company of Lebanese, Palestinians, Syrians, Jordanians, Libyans, and Moroccans, I could prove to others that my identity had some validity. But this term relied on language as the binding component, and I knew only too well that Arabic was spoken with distinct dialects in each of these countries. When I spoke to someone from Lebanon, I smiled and nodded frequently, hoping this was an appropriate response given that I could only grasp about seventy percent of what was being said. While I welcomed this label that placed me in a larger community, it felt like a term created by the need for political solidarity rather than an expression of personal identity.

The events of 9/11 heightened the growing perception of Arabs as terrorists, and I found myself with a new identity to tackle. There was little room here for differentiation among Arabs—the suspicion of terrorism became attached to each of us. Once again, individual identity receded. The perception of my identity had become politicized in negative ways, and there was a new battleground that once again made it difficult to claim a more personal definition.

When I first heard the term Egyptian American being used during the protests, I initially thought: at last, there is space in American culture for me. On the multiple forms that demand we identify ourselves by checking off a predetermined box, I have drawn a square, put a check in it, added a line next to it, and written Egyptian American. The end result is that I'm usually transferred to another box: White, Asian, or African American. Mine is a shifting identity that transforms easily with the winds of politics and perception.

Now I wonder what Egyptian American will mean for most Americans. Will I become a symbol of democratic freedom? At least this has more positive connotations than being perceived as a terrorist, but I'm not sure I can live up to these new expectations. Should I be rehearsing chants to lead the people? Should I be making a list of oppressive governments that must be toppled? Should I be gathering supplies to sustain a resistance movement for eighteen days?

While the protests are happening, a man comes to give us an estimate for remodeling our bathroom. He asks where we are from. My husband remains quiet, knowing the question is for me to answer. "Boston," I respond. "We both grew up in Boston." The man nods. It's difficult to tell if this is the answer he is looking for, something to identify our accents, or if he senses there is more to the story. At the moment, I find myself reluctant to reveal my identity with its new nuances. I'm not quite ready to become a spokesperson for democratic freedom. It will take some time for me to adapt to this new layer of identity.

Supermarket Check-Out

WHILE I'M WAITING IN THE CHECK-OUT LINE at the supermarket, I often occupy myself by spying on the groceries of the person in front of me. I watch others pile their purchases on the conveyer belt, squint my eyes to read the labels of their containers, and wonder at how they will combine their selections to create a meal. I glance back at my own overfilled cart, worried that perhaps my choices are in some way deficient.

It's the beginning of the month, and I'm in the supermarket again, waiting to check out. I look to the man ahead of me—an older man with wrinkles weaving through his face, although his short height and slender physique display the energy of someone much younger. He's wearing a baseball cap that says, "Jesus is My Boss." I watch the items as he places them onto the conveyer belt: Bologna, American cheese, Crisco, Lipton Iced Tea, 36 variety-pack Good Humor ice cream, salsa, bananas, Gatorade, and several bottles of Pine Sol. I survey his selections with jealousy. This man shops like a true American. I imagine him eating a bologna and American cheese sandwich, sitting comfortably in a recliner with a tall glass of Gatorade on the table next to him. His house is spotless, the Pine Sol having done its work, leaving the residue of its smell. This man's purchases float down the conveyer belt with confidence, certain of their identity as the quintessential items of an American shopper. I look down at my own cart: frozen shrimp, smoked salmon, mozzarella cheese, asparagus, garlic, limes, almonds, sparkling apple juice, and fragrance free laundry detergent. In comparison, my choices shrink, revealing their inadequacy.

When I survey other people's items, I take special notice of the pre-packaged foods: pre-made lasagna, just heat and ready to serve; wrapped burritos, just zap in the microwave and eat; cheesecake, just take out of the box and thaw. You'd have to dig deep to find anything pre-cooked in my cart. The cheesecake Celine coerced me into buying two months ago is still taking up space in our freezer. Each of us had a piece, my husband noting that he could taste nothing, Yasmine taking only two bites, and the younger one, who had requested it, complaining of a stomachache as soon as she finished.

When we arrived in 1969, my mother's astonishment at the ready-made food that overflowed from the supermarket aisles led to a myriad of packages filling the small pantry in our rented apartment. At the age of nine, I made my first cake from a Betty Crocker mix. Despite following the directions on the back of the package, my diligence resulted in a cake that collapsed in the middle, as if the effort of creation had deflated it. I scoff at those artificially flavored cake mixes now, although at times I've bought the organic ones for my daughter, wanting to offer her that same sense of quick satisfaction that comes from mixing a few ingredients to find that you have created something solid and whole. Her attempts have yielded greater success, and we have been the lucky recipients of coconut cupcakes, monkey bread, and the plain yellow cake. This is the branch I hold out to those first years of our life in America. We embraced these pre-packaged foods, and when we ate them, it was not the processed flavor that we tasted but the possibility of a new life.

My olive sandwiches on pita bread taken to the Ramses School for Girls transformed into peanut butter sandwiches on Wonder Bread topped off with hostess cupcakes or, my favorite, Ring Dings—the crisp coat of chocolate that surrounded the cake and cream filling satisfying some longing I could not articulate. After school, I pulled down the box from the cabinet to have just one more or perhaps two. These were my indulgences, my search to satisfy a craving that eluded me in those early years of assimilation.

Now I've joined the growing number of healthy shoppers, selecting organic products, going to the farmer's market, and squinting at the list of ingredients to avoid the artificial flavorings and colors. But this man ahead of me makes me question my resolve. There is a cultural frame to his choices, whereas my items seem only a mismatched assortment of products. The only time I can simulate the confidence of his selections is when I go to the small Arab grocery. It's tucked on a side street, although there is a sign on the main street that says "Mediterranean Food"; beneath it in Arabic it says, "The Arab Store"—this mistranslation, heavy with its own political connotations, is perhaps intended to draw in both the American and the Arab customer. I enter this store each month with a full knowledge of where I am. There are no carts or baskets. I grab a few items—Feta cheese, brown lentils, phyllo dough—and place them on the counter then return to the narrow aisles, picking what I desire and putting it alongside my other selections. I open freezers and dig through packages of okra, root vegetables, and frozen falafel to find what I need. There is no reason to ask for help from the young man who sits behind the counter all day watching Arabic sitcoms on his small satellite connected TV. He's from Iraq and our different dialects of Arabic allow only limited conversations, but we understand each other enough.

Along these singular aisles, my confidence is balanced, picking up the rose water for my baklava, the vermicelli for my rice, the lupine beans for Celine, the Arabic gum for my husband, the mango juice for Yasmine, the cumin, the tahini, the *labna*. These ingredients create a clear cultural context for me. The store has a distinct smell like so many ethnic grocery stores in America—a hyphenated odor resulting in an odd disharmony of aroma. It's the smell that makes Yasmine prefer to wait in the car while I go in. Perhaps the clash of flavors agitates her with its awareness of how cultures can repel each other; she prefers the optimism of wholeness, not particles colliding.

When I was a child, my mother dragged me to the supermarket with her. It was a chore I resisted, and I prowled through the aisles behind her, sulking. I realize now that I served as her anchor while she navigated her way through these new products. Her ability to comprehend and embrace this food marked her entrance into American culture, yet it also required her to push aside the Arabic recipe book she had brought with her, its pages smudged with her efforts. This thick compilation with pages threatening to slip out of the spine was the Arabic equivalent of *The Joy of Cooking*, offering the new Egyptian housewife the secret codes to pleasing her family. In the supermarket, my mother would ask my opinions on various products, but I had nothing to contribute—this new culinary world offered little that could tempt my taste buds. I had been raised on fava beans, stuffed zucchini, and kofta—hamburger helper and mashed potatoes in a box that only required adding water couldn't entice me.

After my children were born, I acquired a copy of *The Joy of Cooking*. Its pages have now become unhinged from the spine, and they are marked and spotted by my attempts to master key lime pie, biscuits, and pancakes. This is my doorway into American acculturation. But standing in the supermarket behind this man whose shopping selections exude such confidence, I recognize my own deficiencies. My food selections fall in the category of health conscious, but I've had to adjust to fit myself into this label. The food I grew up with was deep fried or doused with syrup or heaped with fresh cream. And meat was central to each meal. My announcement that I was going to stop eating meat when I was in college was perceived as a betrayal by my family. I have purposely adopted this healthy alternative to eating, but I often find myself balancing uncertainty.

Waiting for this man with his precise collection of food, I'm once again unsettled. I sneak another glance at him as he piles his groceries back into his cart. The hat catches my eye again. The confidence of this man's beliefs displayed on his baseball cap reminds me of the certainty with which my grandmother carried her faith, the purity of her face as Easter approached after forty days of fasting, her willingness to accept the miracle of Christ's rising. I held that same faith through my childhood, fasting according to Coptic tradition by not eating meat and dairy, turning away from all food on Good Friday, and holding close the notion of a higher being. Now I'm left only with a belief in the mystery of our existence.

When I get home, I describe this man to the rest of my family and ask if perhaps this is how I should shop. My children offer nothing in response. They are content with the food they find in their fridge, having categorized me as one of those healthy moms, although they remain confident that I will succumb to the occasional request for marshmallows or pop tarts. My husband, on the other hand, shrugs and says, "Sure, you can shop like that man. I like Good Humor ice cream." His comment sinks me into an abyss of insecurity. I consider bringing home bologna and American cheese, but I know it won't happen. My family will have to remain deprived of these basic American products as I negotiate my way through the aisles of supermarkets. I am unsure whether my husband's comment is serious or an attempt to provoke me. Still, my sense of inadequacy weighs more heavily.

After arriving in America, my parents enrolled me in a Catholic school, and I found myself policed by strict nuns still using the slap of rulers just as we entered the 1970s. The nuns hovered in the cafeteria, guarding the trash cans as we made our way out. I ate hot dogs for the first time and almost choked on the plastic taste creeping down my throat. There was no remnant of flavor that I could hold in my mouth. The nuns reprimanded me for discarding my food. They sent letters home, but my parents agreed with me and ignored the missives accusing me of the sin of wasting food. Ice cream sandwiches equally plagued my taste buds. At each gathering of children, they were offered as dessert, but the cardboard texture that bent into my mouth only called up the bile from my stomach.

Two weeks after my encounter with the man, I retraced my footsteps through the supermarket aisles, having been given the task of providing dessert for Celine's eighth grade class party. I made my way to the freezers at the back the store. My daughters accompanied me to ensure I made an appropriate selection for this American event. I pointed to the all-natural fruit bars. They shook their heads. Seeing my disappointment, they suggested maybe I could get them for the adults. Then they directed their attention to the ice cream sandwiches and Good Humor ice cream. I drooped in front of the freezer in the middle of this supermarket with its concrete floors and fluorescent-lit ceilings. I looked again at the fruit bars, but my American children shook their heads. My options narrowed, and I dutifully followed their instructions, leaving with one family-size box of ice cream sandwiches and one variety pack of Good Humor ice cream.

We made our way to the checkout where we placed our purchases on the conveyer belt. I glanced at my daughters and saw their content faces. The items moved forward and I let them, knowing that I could make enough room for them in my life.

After the Egyptian Revolution

I'M SIX OR SEVEN YEARS OLD. We're sitting in the living room and we have guests. I'm crouched on the floor next to my grandmother, leaning against her. An only child, I'm often part of adult gatherings. I'm allowed to listen, but never to repeat what I hear. It's the 1960s in Egypt, and some words have the power to make you disappear. This is what I've been told, so I've learned to take in words and hold them tight. But something in this conversation must've disturbed my silence as I tried to make sense of the tangle of adult language. I tug at my grandmother's dress and she bends toward me. In her ear, I whisper my question: "Does this mean that all Muslims will go to hell?" My grandmother, who explains the world to me each day, puts her finger on her lips and says, "Shhh, don't ask such questions." I realize that I've stumbled into a forbidden place, a place that my grandmother's Bible stories can't explain, a place that language can't decipher, a place that even adults are not allowed to enter.

**

It's August 2013 and Egypt has erupted in violence. I try to turn away from the news, as if my avoidance could erase the headlines. My husband throws me nuggets of information: "82 people died," "they're calling for a march to show support for the military," "a state of emergency is going to be declared." I watch the water boil for pasta, I stir the green beans, I turn over the chicken in the oven, letting his words evaporate into the smoke rising in my kitchen. But at some point, the news tugs too strongly and I settle into it, defeated.

**

Only a few weeks earlier, I had posted the pictures and information coming in about the people's march against Mohamed Morsi, the president of Egypt elected after the Egyptian Revolution that occurred in 2011. Thirty-three million, maybe as many as forty million, marched in the streets demanding an end to Morsi's regime. Trying to counteract the U.S. news that presented it as an uprising against democracy, I participated in showing this was the will of the people. After a year in office, Morsi and the Muslim Brotherhood had not helped the country to move forward. I didn't understand the nuances of the political decisions being made by his government, but I knew from everyone I talked to in Egypt that those decisions were not acceptable to the majority of Egyptians. There is no impeachment process in Egypt. What exists, now after the 2011 revolution, are the demands of the people as expressed by their willingness to march in the streets. And half the population of Egypt had made their voices heard by gathering to insist on Morsi stepping down.

What I could not wrap my mind around was what happened after the military carried out the demands of the people and forced Morsi out: the dehumanization and resulting justification of the violence perpetrated against the Brotherhood or anyone near them, the burning of churches and government buildings by Morsi supporters, the number of people dying. I'm disturbed by the violence on both sides combined with the anti-American propaganda emerging from Egypt, portraying the American government as supporters of the Muslim Brotherhood and the enemy of Egypt, accusing Obama of giving aid to a terrorist organization—these contradictory political manipulations press against me, pushing me into contorted positions of discomfort as I try to resist being drawn into any side of the equation forming.

***

I was in elementary school in the early 1970s when the Vietnam War was still going on. Someone asked me which side I would fight on if America was at war with Egypt: to choose between my birth country where much of my family still lived and the country where I was now building a future. I shrugged my shoulders in response, but the question settled inside me. After 9/11, the same tug of war hovered above America as patriotism loomed with flags flying out of car windows. One radio announcer said what many may have been thinking: "There is no place for a hyphenated American."

I settle myself on that hyphen, looking in both directions.

***

The Egyptian military and the people standing with them have declared the Muslim Brotherhood to be a terrorist organization. Quotes, pictures, and articles swarm the internet relaying the number of churches that have been burned, the buildings destroyed, the people attacked by the Brotherhood. I call my aunt who lives in Old Cairo surrounded by some of the oldest Coptic churches. She tells me they are all well. The churches are fine; nothing has been burned. Someone posts that there is no security around the churches that have been destroyed, mostly in Upper Egypt, insinuating that the military is allowing this to happen in order to increase the hostility against the Brotherhood.

***

In America, the classroom driving instructor approaches my daughter, Celine: "And where are you from?" Caught off guard by his tone of accusation, she gives her standard response: my mother is from Egypt and my father is African American. He catches only the Egyptian part and replies, "Oh, I got to talk to you." Learning that her Egyptian family is Christian, he charges into a monologue, asserting that the Christians are ok but not "those dam Muslim Turks with the pressure cooker bomb and those Muslim women who can't talk to anyone."

***

The word terrorist drops like a heavy lump. This word has pushed itself into American life, carried by the portrayal of Palestinians fighting for their homeland, and it has been stretched like a thin gauze to cover every Arab American after the 9/11 attacks. Seeing it tossed so easily in the rhetoric of the Egyptian military makes me uneasy, and I feel a need to dissect it, to understand what is inside of this word whose impact as an Arab American I have felt. "What is a terrorist?" I ask my family at dinner that night. —*Someone who does violent acts, but they're motivated by a political belief; the violence is wrong, but they're doing it because they believe in something*— The killing in Egypt is being justified with the label terrorist: killing without trial done in the streets, indiscriminately, and anyone who is killed is labeled a terrorist so their murder will not be questioned, even those who are caught in the midst of the mayhem unintentionally. What future is possible now?

***

A curfew has been imposed by the military from seven in the evening to six in the morning. Cairo's streets are always brimming with people, especially at night when the air cools. It's hard to imagine the city shut down, its streets empty, and in complete quiet. Some say the curfew is meant to camouflage the violence taking place.

***

It is estimated that about 1000 people have died. Over thirty men in a truck being taken to prison were gassed. There is not enough room in the morgues, and bodies are being stored in freezer trucks. Who is dying?—someone accidently in the wrong place, someone helping a wounded friend—what can be built on this foundation? The distance from my homeland widens into a chasm that I can no longer cross.

***

I remember my daughters at the age of six and three watching a movie together. When my three year old gets scared of what's happening in the movie, my older daughter comforts her, assuring her that "the good guys always win."

***

I'm following my cousin's posts on Facebook. Born and raised in the U.S., he's been living in Egypt for a number of years. His political perspective gives me a better balance of what's happening. But what catches my attention are his posts about trying to get food delivered from the various restaurants after curfew. Sushi is available, he posts one evening. Another day, a different restaurant is delivering. And a recent post says that he saw a delivery person after curfew stopping a police officer to ask for directions. Perhaps this is the key to survival in Egypt. Maneuvering around the rules to find an alternate route, like the traffic that makes its way through the maze of Cairo's streets, oblivious to the few lights that continue to blink on and off. Against such obstacles, there is the eternal desire to keep moving and to keep eating. Cairo resists this shut down, and those who persist in living beyond the curfew give me some hope—to imagine a future where I can return to my homeland, walk its streets, breathe the spirit of its generosity.

Motherhood -
Mangos, Papayas
&
Classic Hummus

It's Saturday and I'm at Sam's Club, my least favorite day to come here with the crowds of shoppers clogging the aisles, reaching for the oversized bags of chicken wings and stacks of uniformly shaped hamburgers. If there are tastings set up, those small stands staffed by mostly elderly women who offer you a half-bite size of breaded chicken or a scrape of salsa on a chip, then the super large shopping carts congeal into these areas as customers wait for the slow and methodical cooking to yield an offer of free food. But we're out of toilet paper, laundry detergent, and tissues, and the prices for these bulk items at Sam's Club entice me each month, as well as the hope that buying in large quantities will mean fewer trips to the grocery store. Along the way, I'm picking up the items I get each month—shrimp, green beans, goat cheese. I'm a picky shopper, the one who stands in the aisle reading the ingredients on the package.

Today, I'm trying to zigzag my way through the store and around the multitude of carts. I head down the last aisle of the frozen section, which is usually not as crowded, just to catch my breath and decide what else I need to get. "Hello Yasmine's mother." A voice catches my ear, and I look away from my reflection in the frozen glass. It's a young woman and presumably her mother who also seem to be taking some respite from the crowds in this last aisle of the store. "I'm Shaquanda," the young woman says in response to my befuddled look, "Jamila's cousin." I put it together: the cousin of my older daughter's friend whom I have met once before. But I'm struck by the way I've been identified—"Yasmine's mother"—the mother of Yasmine. This is how I would've been known if I had remained in Egypt, my identity as a woman re-packaged after giving birth. Traditionally, the term *Umm*, "mother" or "mother of," is followed by the son's name, used as an expression of pride and accomplishment for women who have given birth to sons. Now, it seems a greater element of equality has entered the culture as I've heard the term followed by the daughter's name when there are no sons. I'm transported out of Sam's Club by Shaquanda's call to me, taken to my uncle's home in Cairo, where he fondly refers me to as "Umm Yasmine." "Hello," I finally respond, and we stop to chat for a few moments before we continue our journey through the maze.

I make my way to the fruits and vegetables: garlic, grape tomatoes, limes. I notice the mangoes placed between the kiwis and papayas; the open cardboard boxes piled on top of each other have been rummaged through, and only a few still display six pieces of fruit lined up neatly. The mangoes have spilled out, creating a disorderly arrangement. I approach the mountain and proceed to create my own box, selecting the fruit that appears to be at a good stage of ripeness. When my parents and I arrived in America at the end of 1969, there were no mangoes in the grocery stores—or pomegranates or feta cheese—and even molasses was difficult to find, at least in the northeast. Our taste for these items receded, and we learned to crave the hard texture of granny smith apples and the juiciness of navel oranges. Now mangoes and even pomegranates have arrived at Sam's Club. But there are other tastes that remain elusive, their memory sometimes slipping across my tongue: the soft pitted sweetness of a guava, the textured bite of a prickly pear, and the edged sugar of a yellow date.

I'm engrossed in the task of selecting my mangoes when suddenly I realize there is a woman peering over my shoulder, barely inches away. As soon as she senses my awareness of her, she blurts out, "How do you eat those?" I'm caught off guard as I stumble for an answer. There is more than one way to eat a mango and the possibilities jumble in my mind, but I give her my most instinctive answer—you cut each side off, then you slice squares into each one and pop them up to eat. This is the way my grandmother cut them for me when I was a child, and it is the way I cut them for my daughters who eat them, slurping the juice that slides down their chins just as I did. The woman's perplexed look makes me realize this is too complicated, so I try to retrieve my answer, adding, "You can just peel them and slice them." But it's too late, and she responds that maybe she'll try them some other time. I return with my box of carefully chosen mangoes to my cart, feeling like somehow I have failed. But it's only a moment before the woman is tapping me on the shoulder, holding a papaya in her hand. "What are these?" she asks me. I realize that I have been designated an expert on "exotic" fruit and wonder how I have earned this distinction. Is it the way I was eyeing each mango as I made my selection or is it my black hair and darker complexion. "It's a papaya," I answer and before she can ask, I explain, "You cut it in half and scoop out the seeds then you can peel and slice it, like a cantaloupe or melon." This seems to satisfy her. "Is this a good one?" she asks, offering the large fruit for my approval. I know little about choosing papayas, but I examine it and assure her that it's ideal.

This is perhaps not the first time my advice has been sought in a supermarket. Usually, it happens by the watermelons. I lean over the large cardboard container, tapping each melon and listen carefully to the sound that resonates. Passersby will either ignore me or give me a quizzical look. Occasionally, someone will stop and inquire, "How can you tell?" I explain that the sound of the melon should echo, not be flat. But it's a hard translation to make; the literal meaning is that the sound should *ring*. I don't know how to explain this, but I can hear it. Everyone taps watermelons in Egypt. If you stop someone selling watermelons on a cart in the street, they will tap it for you, asserting the ripeness of their fruit by the distinctive tone that everyone can recognize. Here, I'm left with my limited knowledge of papayas. But the woman smiles at my reassurance, and she is off with her purchase. I can only hope that this small step she is taking into the world of unknown fruits will yield happiness.

My journey continues toward the cheese, and I purchase my usual supersize chunk of cheddar along with a double package of mozzarella. I decide against the frozen ravioli, then turn the corner to the pizzas, but as my eyes skim over the circular layers, I'm caught by a new product. Piled in pyramid shape are large round plastic tubs labeled "Classic Hummus"; they are oversized containers and once again I'm in awe of Sam's Club's ability to package everything in giant bulk size. No one had heard of hummus when we first arrived, one of the most staple foods in the Middle East. Hummus is common in Lebanon and Palestine. In Egypt, there is the *tahini* dip, a lighter mixture since it doesn't contain any chickpeas. The popularity of hummus has increased rapidly over the past ten years. But this is not quite the hummus of the Middle East, which is a basic dip served with pita bread. At Taboula, the Lebanese restaurant where we frequently ate the last time we were in Egypt, they served hummus in three ways: plain, garnished with a tomato mixture, or topped with meat. But like other immigrant foods, hummus has acquired a new identity since its arrival in America, or more accurately several new identities, suggesting hints of schizophrenia. Hummus now comes in an assortment of flavors, including Horseradish, Cilantro, Tomato & Basil, Caramelized Onion, Cranberry and Fig, Sun Dried Tomatoes, and Spinach Artichoke. I must admit that I have bought some of these flavors and enjoyed them, although I feel a sense of betrayal as I dip each piece of pita bread into the smooth ready-made mixture that combines new flavors for my taste buds. I also feel guilty for buying it rather than making it myself. But when I stand in front of the refrigerator section at the supermarket weighing my guilt, I picture myself at home, scraping the slippery sesame paste out of the jar and into the blender, adding the watery chickpeas, peeling the resistant garlic, squeezing the stinging limes, and, in the process, creating an unsightly and sticky mess on my kitchen counter. Inevitably, the small plastic container offering its myriad of flavors looks far more appealing.

This is America, always in search of the new and unusual. In the Middle East, we are more predictable, and you can be assured that even our food will come with a side order of politics. The ongoing battle between Lebanon and Israel about who owns the right to hummus provides sufficient proof. Lebanon has accused Israeli companies of marketing hummus and labeling it as an Israeli product, claiming that hummus belongs to Lebanon. Ownership of food is a sensitive issue in the Middle East. If you ask me where baklava comes from as I'm offering you a piece from the tray I took out of the oven that morning filled with pistachios and dripping with honey, my answer will be Egypt. If you attempt to argue with me and mention Greece or Turkey, you will find yourself standing with an empty plate.

The seriousness of claiming the cultural identity of food came to a climactic moment in May 2010 as Lebanon and Israel vied for their ownership of hummus by competing for the Guinness world record for making the biggest vat of hummus. Three hundred Lebanese chefs prepared a bowl of hummus weighing over eleven tons in downtown Beirut in order to win the world record. The title was previously held by Israel, an achievement that brought them closer to claiming ownership over this dip whose popularity has reached international status. But this year, the determination of the Lebanese was clear. The videos show each chef presiding over his individual bowl, mixing and stirring it into a creamy concoction. Their combined efforts succeeded, and the Lebanese won, decorating their giant size bowl of hummus with Lebanese flags. Celine brought in the article for show and share. Her teacher asked what was next—*falafel?* Actually, Lebanon has already won that record by making over 11,000 pounds of falafel. The next battle will determine who can make the largest plate of *tabouleh.*

I try to step away from the hummus, but my eye catches the brand name—Sabra. My sight stretches beyond the display: Sabra and Shatila are two refugee camps in the outskirts of Beirut that were attacked during the

1982 Israeli invasion of Lebanon. Israeli forces controlled the area, while allowing the Phalangist militia to enter the camps. It is estimated that as many as 2000 Palestinian civilians were killed during the massacres. The giant size tubs of hummus, made by the Israeli Sabra Dipping Company, sit calmly in the middle of Sam's Club where no one is likely to connect them to this history. News of the destruction of Palestinian refugee camps doesn't travel to America. When I returned from Egypt in the summer of 2002, I tried to talk about what had happened in Jenin, a refugee camp in the West Bank that the Israeli Defense Forces had attacked: they entered with armored bull-dozers and destroyed homes with people still inside. Israel declared Jenin a "closed military zone," and it remained sealed throughout the invasion. No humanitarian aid was allowed into the camp. But no one in the U.S. had heard anything about Jenin, and I swallowed back the history of what I knew.

A man wanders up to the containers of hummus and looks at them for a minute, then turns away. Other shoppers make their way around me, as if I were another product display. I feel more alienated from American culture than when people start talking about music or old actors. My difference is a line of vision through these tubs of hummus that no one else can see. I leave the oversized containers behind—I know I have to move on. But it's clear that my shopping expedition has come to an end and I head toward the cashiers. Today, I've forgotten to bring my assortment of shopping bags with me, and the cashier piles my purchases into the cart, a mismatched assortment of items that the check person at the door looks over before marking a yellow line down my receipt.

Outside there is a steady drizzle. I push my overloaded cart toward my usual parking spot. Once again, my trusty Volvo station wagon's trunk door refuses to stay up. With one hand, I hold it, as I situate my foot behind one of the front wheels of the cart to keep it from rolling away into the endless parking lot. That leaves one hand with which to transport each of my items from the cart to the trunk. I juggle this precarious act rather well as the rain continues its persistent descent. Things are moving along until I reach for the box of mangos. It's heavy and hard to balance with one hand. As I attempt to transport it, its weight dips and the box slips out of my grasp. Half of my carefully selected mangos tumble out and roll beneath the car. I put the half-empty box in the trunk, let go of the door, and kneel on the wet pavement. One by one, I reach for each mango, retrieving them. They have rolled in different directions, and I have to re-situate my position and stretch my arm's length to bring them back. Mangoes are a hardy fruit, and I know they will survive this tumble; each one will still be savored. This awkward retrieval is necessary, I think, as the wet rain soaks into my pants. Other shoppers glance at my unexpected posture, but I persist, here in this place, kneeling in worship of these mangos. Some things cannot be lost.

The History of My Accent

The accent's energy follows a different tempo proper to the
mother tongue, and when the voice carries it into a foreign
language, the result is an illusion of an attempt to speak two
languages at the same instant, one on the surface and the
other concealed, one in motion and the other sidelined, up
in arms at its neglect and abandonment.
    —Iman Mersal, *"The Displaced Voice"*

"ARE YOU FROM ENGLAND? You sound like you have a London accent."
The man behind the counter who asks me this owns the best bakery in
town. His scones entice me each time I enter the small shop—chocolate and
hazelnut, orange and ginger, cinnamon and raisin. I confess I'm capable of
eating the entire scone at a single sitting. By 10:00 am, the small nourishment
of my morning bowl of cereal leaves my stomach hollow, lunch is too distant
a promise, and that scone in its buttery softness with the unexpected bitter-
sweet of chocolate is the only thing that can subdue desire.

His question is polite, sincere, and after all, you could say we know each
other, what with our conversations about the merits of good cooking, French
pastries, and the lack of decent bakeries in this small city—although usually
he's talking and I'm eyeing the baked goods, deciding between the brioche,
the shortbread, or that scrumptious crispy sugar and butter French thing
whose name I can't pronounce that sits behind the glass in complete deca-
dence, exhibiting itself as the manifestation of temptation.

"No," I answer reluctantly, almost wishing I could claim the British Empire
for my identity. I go on to explain that as a child growing up in Egypt, I
attended a British school and picked up the accent. After immigrating to the
United States and gathering the accents of various regions where I've lived, that
insistent British accent still sneaks up occasionally on both me and my listener.

My words twist back to the memory of my first learned English pronunciations—
teachers imported from Britain, instilling the legacy of a colonial education to
Egyptian children. Their proper pronunciation and insistence on our strict imita-

tion crawled beneath the layers of my skin. The rules of spelling and grammar remain so ingrained that each school paper I write during my first years in America is returned with the sharpness of red marks, crossing out "ou" spellings and correcting commas outside of quotation marks.

For some reason, it pleases me when that hint of a British accent is recognized. Perhaps it takes me back to the nostalgia of my childhood spent in the security of my extended family; perhaps it makes me feel larger, my footprints extending across continents; or perhaps I'm as infatuated as most Americans with the sound of that British lilt. The problem with that accent is that I can't voluntarily call it up; if I try, what emerges is as silly as a mouth full of Pop Rocks. Instead, it emerges at unexpected moments like this morning in the bakery, summoned perhaps by the sweet smell of scones.

***

Boston is a nasal twang, words running together with no pause for breath, each syllable chasing the other till they tumble into an indistinguishable pile of broken sounds. Meaning turns into a traffic jam in my ears, so I practice a nod, a half smile in response. In my fourth grade class, instructions float to the fluorescent ceiling. I write my name at the top of each assignment, leaving everything else blank, and then hand it back to the teacher who will have only empty spaces to mark. I exist inside my own head, where there is no language to bind my thoughts. I'm eight years old, and it will take me six months to untangle the snarl of this new language, one thread at a time like a necklace knotted tight from sitting crumbled at the bottom of a jewelry box. The words will connect into intricacies of sound and meaning, as I move toward listening and finally uttering sound.

"Say 'the rabbit ran'."

My junior high school classmates fling this demand at me. Their order wavers between ridicule and an attempt to help. The letter *r* twists in my mouth, its sound leaning toward *w*. I can't quite master the roll of the tongue required to send out that ring. By the time the words emerge, my cars have turned into cows, taking over city streets and making their way to unknown destinations.

My classmates and I are climbing up the long hilly sidewalks between our school and our suburban homes. I'm the first Egyptian any of them have encountered, and the justification for my garbled speech is assumed by all of us to be my origin in this land they've only seen in the photograph of pyramids and camels inserted into their history books. These classmates are the closest thing I have to friends after four years in America. They snicker at my pronunciation, but their attempt to correct me implies some kindness that I'm willing to accept. The hill becomes heavy on those humid summer days, and our huffing breath makes us pause. It's a long climb after a day of school, but at least I'm not alone and their company wraps me in the illusion of friendship.

Our walk home becomes a lesson in speech therapy, and my young teachers delight in my progress, although there is little of it. I watch the movement of their tongues, but I'm never able to master that trill of the *r*. I only learn to corral my cows and substitute the word automobile. I vow to marry a man whose name does not contain this devious letter and to remove all trace of it in the names I pick for my children. I want to call the ones I love by the full sounds of their names.

For years, I assume that my broken *r*s are a result of being a native Arabic speaker. But as I get older, I hear my mother's voice ride through the letter *r* with a perfect ringtone of music. Then I detect the subtle way my father falters over the sound. It's barely perceptible, not as obvious as my own, but it's still there, that *w* sneaking in behind the *r*, insisting on earning a more visible place. It has nothing to do with first and second languages, just an inherited twist of tongue unable to perform the necessary gymnastics to release the correct sound. Perhaps it's easier, more exotic to claim it as an accent carried through the transition of languages.

My classmates have better luck with my *a*s. "It's not J*aa*mes. It's J*ae*mes," they teach me. My *a*s stand up straight, their back aligned against the letter that precedes them. They're tall, proud of their contribution to each word. But my classmates tell me that most *a*s want to lean back, reclining against other letters. I tilt my head to follow their example, as if I could push that *a* onto its side. Eventually, the practice of repetition as we climb the hill each day works; I've mastered the *a*, and there is one less thing to distinguish me from others in this new world.

***

Michigan is a slow walk, taking its time, letting each sound have its space like the expanse of wheat fields. Vowels and consonants spread out and let the wind catch them like cotton tails swaying in the summer. Language is an even land-

scape, flat land where you can see far into the distance, an endless vista. My ears are lulled by the even tones of this music where I can link the thread of sounds to make meaning. My own words begin to flatten, an even tone to decipher this quiet movement. I'm a graduate student, initially uncertain about my place here, but slowly I begin to unfold and find space where I can blend into this Midwest summer breeze.

It's mid-afternoon and I'm on my way to class, occupied in my own thoughts. I've learned to walk fast in this Midwestern college town. My dark skin and the twang of my Boston accent label my difference. Every time I stop, I have to explain myself, and the wide-eyed response frames and hangs me as an exotic specimen. Three young men walk past me, and I sense their glance in my direction. They pass me by a few feet, then stop and turn to block my movement. "What are you?" One of them fires the question at me. I try to side-step around them. "C'mon," he persists, "what are you?" I'm edging off the sidewalk into the street as his voice barrels at me: "Puerto Rican? Italian? Mexican?" Anything could inflame this encounter. I wrap my body and my voice in silence.

***

Egypt is a ping-pong of call and response, words snapped back and forth against crowded sidewalks, traffic jams, tall buildings, and cluttered store fronts. A sharp game that requires the memorization of sound and rhythm learned from child-hood. A guttural song that flies across these streets of home. But my reflexes are out of practice and I'm a beat too slow, my rhythm off by a notch, so I'm iden-tified from elsewhere: Algeria, Palestine, Lebanon. My ears readjust and listen to language moving across this landscape of noise, maneuvering its way through obstacles. Sprinkles of English and French dot like accent marks over the Arabic that congregates through city streets. A history of conquerors and resistance inter-spersed like a battling orchestra to claim space in this crowded city turning into a conglomeration of intertwining sounds that elevate above this myriad landscape. Two weeks after returning, I dream in the language of my first sounds, retrieved from early memories until the pattern of pitch and tone is recaptured. Arabic letters demand the movement of lips and tongue (no silent letters), each word enunciated, that guttural flexing of muscle in throat and diaphragm, a sound hitting pavement. Each syllable requires the full body's utterance pronounced in clear pitch. Nothing mumbled here. It's the desert opening into unexpected oasis.

It's the love songs where each longing word sung by Umm Kalthoum extends as long as the Nile. It's the evening sun descending onto the Mediterranean that cradles the urban shore where sound resurrects from throat to claim this land. With language, memory of body returns, so my walk down Cairo streets shifts to the music of traffic and speech until I'm blended into landscape of home and no one asks where I'm from.

"When you talk to your mom, you speak with an accent."

Celine announces this after overhearing my conversation with my mother on the phone. I had never realized that I spoke with an accent among my family until my daughters pointed it out.

Most of my aunts and uncles emigrated, following my parents who began the family exodus in 1969. They all arrived in their thirties, ready to take on the challenge of living in this new world. Hard work and perseverance they expected, but it was the weight of language they didn't anticipate. The *ths* and the *ps* trapped their tongues, raising the pitch of their voices as they practiced these new pronunciations, like an old person learning to plié for the first time, the limbs unaccustomed to the bend and stretch of muscle.

When my family gets together, we all talk at the same time, our chatter rising above the aroma of my mother's pot roast and grape leaves. The pitch fluctuates from baritone to alto, and each sound is a single note, distinct and tight, given its full weight. Only the occasional sprinkle of an English word rises to soprano, accentuating the conversation. Alone, I can't imitate someone who speaks English with an Arabic accent, yet I've grown up around that tilt of language since the age of eight. But when I'm with my relatives or on the phone with them, my voice shifts and years of imbibing American English disappear. I'm not the woman with a PhD in English who has published books and corrects the faults in student papers. That immigrant haunting of English as a second language finds my tongue, and I slip into an accent that stumbles over rocks and branches on a wooded path.

Like all second-generation children, my daughters are able to imitate the accent of Arab immigrants on demand. They can emulate those chipped sounds, yet my tongue, caught as a one-and-a half generation immigrant, catches it only when I'm inside a conversation with a true native speaker.

***

Upstate New York is mountains rolling into valleys that open to unexpected gorges and waterfalls. New York City accents harmonize against a back-

ground of rhythms that match the moving landscape. I hear that distinctive urban dialect born of a city of immigrants crossing each other's paths to carve out new spaces of identity. It's an amalgamation of high and low pitches, of sound travelling across water; each person carries their history in their speech, and I find a place here for my own mixed ancestry of language and dialect. I'm another voice in this landscape that stretches itself back to other continents across oceans. Each rolling mountain dips into a valley until it reaches water that nurtures with its abundance of dialects that rise and fall—emotion held at the tip of the tongue to pour out a land that remains in constant motion.

I'm browsing in a shoe store in downtown Roanoke, VA, and I notice a middle-aged couple giggling as they try on the new toe shoes that have a separate space for each toe. I comment that my husband recently bought a pair. We exchange a few words and the man asks where I'm from. I hesitate, but the man quickly responds to his own question, telling me, "You're from New York, but not the city." His exact guess of the last place I lived catches me off guard. "He's very good at that," his wife says, as if to calm my fear at being so precisely placed in the world. When I mention that I'm originally from Egypt and that I have lived in Boston and the Midwest, he expresses little interest. He has already defined me by the identity I carry in my most recent words. I lived in upstate New York for only five years, yet it's this last trace that has caught his ear, making me wonder if I could claim this as my rightful location.

***

Southwest Virginia is an obstacle course. I trip and catch my fall as I try to speak. My foreignness here is the region of my sound. I'm unable to hide the northern twist of my tongue that betrays me; it's not only sound but the angle of my speech—greetings and relationships that take their time, the "Ma'am" and "Sir" that catch me unawares, the small talk before business, the hold the door for strangers. I have to slow my movement, not only the slur of my speech. There are mountains here that rise higher, stretching to peaks that can catch snow, and the valley I'm in is surrounded with no break for water. It's the slow descent of coming down from a mountain and the rest after the climb that marks this speech pattern. It takes me longer to catch the rhythm of this landscape. The "y'all" that encompasses a community, the careful step-dance of greeting. I find the walk of sound easier when I recognize this landscape as a reminder of my first home far away, matching the long stretch of desert and Nile water. And slowly I begin to meander a path through this region I choose to call home.

"Where are you from?"

I've just met someone. It's perhaps two minutes into our conversation before the question is presented to me. I've recently moved to Virginia, but it doesn't matter. Wherever I live in this country, the question seems inevitable.

"I'm from Egypt," I respond.

But there is no acknowledgment on this person's face. Only a puzzled look as if I've given the wrong answer on a multiple choice test.

"I mean your accent"—he attempts to elaborate—"Are you from up North?"

"Yes, I'm from Boston," I offer.

"Ohhh," he responds, the confusion clearing.

In Virginia, I've learned that region can take precedence over ethnicity. In the north, people needed a label to make sense of my appearance; here, it's the placement of my accent within an American context that others need to decipher.

***

"Mom, say enthusiasm again."

Celine says this with her lips slipping into a smirk.

I've been caught again, the weight of my linguistic history betraying me and eliciting the ridicule that can only come from a teenage child.

"No," I answer.

"Please," she says, lengthening the word as if she were five and asking for ice cream. I can still detect the squirm at the side of her mouth that she can't quite hide.

"You need to put away your laundry." I give my parental order.

What is it about that word? The double *s* following the *th* must be tripping my tongue in some way. *Th* is one of those sounds that always gives away the Arabic native speaker. That *t* and *h* combine forces that make us falter. There is the letter *theh* in Arabic, which seemingly parallels the *th* sound but *theh* doesn't vibrate the tongue, whereas *th* sends a slight tremor like the sensation of your foot moving after falling asleep. I trip over these sounds, and every time I say the word, I sense the letter *z* trying to sneak in. Unlike those who immigrated at an older age, I can articulate the sound *th* correctly in every other English word. With this word, my tongue abandons me and reveals my true identity.

My daughter catches me each time, pulling at my vulnerability to expose the layer beneath the surface of my educated appearance. I've worked hard to create my linguistic mask, molding it with care as I practiced each sound I heard, trying to differentiate myself from that older immigrant generation who could never camouflage their identity. Their displacement in this new world revealed itself in more than language, the articulated gestures of their hands moving while speaking, their befuddlement at Chinese restaurant menus, their confusion at the nuances of small talk. I figured out how to carefully fold, crease, and tuck away those elements of a past identity that no longer had a place. But here is my daughter unpacking what I have so diligently put away, revealing the frayed edges of my first self.

Words that still make me stumble: probably, parable, palpable. The ps and bs numb my tongue. No p in Arabic, only the letter b with its hard vibration. Distinguishing between these two sounds—I exist inside both languages.

Celine remains insistent, and I decide to oblige her. I repeat the word "enthusiasm," allowing her laughter to bring out my own. These remnants tug at my words, but at times, I prefer to swallow those years of working so hard to remove the traces of an accent and instead return to the vowels and consonants of that first language, letting it slip into my carefully earned English, to remind my tongue of its ancestry.

A Sense of Direction

MY HUSBAND CLAIMS I HAVE A BAD SENSE OF DIRECTION. He presents the following evidence:

- The belief that whenever we find ourselves at an intersection trying to determine whether our destination is to the right or left, the turn I suggest is inevitably the wrong one. This gives my husband the pleasure of saying he was right—an accomplishment he rarely achieves.
- The story I told him about driving to a job interview in a small town in southern Massachusetts only to be confronted with the "Welcome to Rhode Island" sign. My attempts to convince him that this was simply a premature welcome to the small state where we would one day live have failed.
- The fact that my method of driving requires me to take the longest route to my destination. I don't like driving on highways, which I define as any road with a speed limit above thirty-five.

I remind my husband that the responsibility for my fear of highways is a direct result of misplaced confidence in his directional abilities. When we did move to Rhode Island, we had to transport some of our belonging from his parents' house in Massachusetts to our new home in Providence. I followed him as we drove back to Boston, navigating the myriad highways and the drivers who calculate two inches as a sufficient amount of space between their car and yours. As we approached our exit on the right, my husband signaled to move into the left lane. My instincts told me this wasn't right, and I remained in my lane, trying to communicate telepathically with him. He didn't budge, so I suppressed my instincts and switched lanes to get behind him. Two seconds before the exit, he switched back to the right and took the exit. It was too late for me to follow him, and I found myself on a five lane highway in the middle of Boston during rush hour. By the time I managed to get out of the steaming traffic, I had vowed never to drive on a highway again.

My husband needs to believe that he knows where he's going, even when he doesn't. The advent of the GPS has done little to help the situation—he argues with Carmen, as we fondly call our GPS, and claims she's telling him the wrong way. My daughters have surrendered their social lives after spending an hour in the car while my husband drives, trying to get them to a friend's house for a party, claiming he knows where it is when he has been going in the opposite direction.

***

I may have acquired my sense of direction from my parents. When we immigrated in 1969, the plane tickets clearly listed Los Angeles as our destination, yet we ended up in Boston.

My parents' failed attempt to make it to our original destination may have resulted from the difficulty of transitioning from the Arabic speaking world to the English one. Arabic moves from right to left, and this serves to establish our sense of direction from the moment we perceive the written language. After spending six months in Cairo, this movement became so ingrained in my children that when they returned to America, they flipped their books and notebooks around and to the other side so the pages could turn in the direction of Arabic. When I arrived in America at the age of eight, learning to go from left to right with the English language must've permanently damaged my ability to move in a straight line. Given a choice, I'm most likely to turn right, moving back to the origin of the first language I learned.

I have lived in Michigan, New York, Rhode Island, and Virginia, but the West Coast still eludes me. Now, both my daughters are applying to colleges in California—perhaps they have retrieved those original tickets.

***

I never panic when I lose my way. My faith remains unshaken—if I keep walking or driving, I know I will end up in the right direction. It's only when we get lost that we find our destination. I present the following evidence:

- We are young, spending a month backpacking in Europe. The heat from the sun subsides as we meander through the narrow corridors of Venice. There is a continuity of architecture that makes it difficult to decipher one street from another, and we can't be sure if we have already walked this way. We are lost. My husband's nerves become agitated; he's eager to find some sign in this urban forest to guide us back to our hotel. *Don't worry*, I assure him, *if we just keep walking, we'll find our way*. But he's impatient, unable to enjoy the scenery of this city framed by water. There is nothing he can hold onto, so he lets me lead, and my footsteps carry us from one turn to the next. The sun is setting and a gray light envelops the small city. The approaching dark heightens my husband's anxiety, and he's even willing to ask someone. At one turn, we come face to face with a group of travelers, but they are also lost and have no direction to offer us. The sun descends as we make another turn and find ourselves standing in front of our hotel.

• We are in Martinique. My husband has received a grant to pursue his research on the Martiniquan writer, Aimé Césaire. When I ask him if he'll try to meet Césaire while we're in Martinique, he says he'll just see if it happens. My husband is definitely not a planner. A few days into our trip, we're standing on a street corner, about to embark on an afternoon walk. The plan is to go in the direction of a garden we've read about. *I think it's to the left*, my husband says. *No*, I respond, *I think we go straight down that street.* Our two daughters stand between us, unsure of which parent to trust. My husband acquiesces, perhaps hoping to revel in proving me wrong. We walk alongside fan palm trees and hibiscus flowers in this island vibrant with colors and people who move with firm footsteps. Yasmine notices a large building with a sign indicating that it's a theatre. Her love of drama enables her to find her way to a stage even in foreign lands. We enter into the building, my husband immediately noticing the numerous posters of Césaire. We wander up the steps to discover that the second floor holds the offices of Aimé Césaire. Asking a few casual questions of a woman sitting behind a desk, my husband finds himself with an appointment to meet Césaire the next day.

My sense of direction eludes the logic of someone like my husband who takes the most direct route from Point A to Point B. I tell him that there is more than one way to get to your destination—side streets and zigzag turns that can lead you to unexpected places as you travel. Perhaps it's the history that brought his ancestors from Africa to the shores of America that makes him resistant to my logic. Such history demands a clear sense of direction— the ability to trace the path back to your origins, to find the trail that moves North, to carry a drum beat from one ear to another—a triangulation of lines that must be followed for survival.

***

I cannot deny that my husband is correct when he says I can get lost anywhere. Once I step outside my door, there is no way to know where I will end up. I might take a right instead of a left; I might let my curiosity guide me down a street I've never been; or I might decide to lengthen my walk by making a circle that inevitably doesn't lead back to my starting point. My ability to get lost solidified during my study abroad trip to Oxford during the summer of my junior year in college. I didn't know the other students and often found myself with extra time. On days with no classes, I took the bus to London alone. When I got to the city, I walked. I didn't visit any museums or historical sites. Instead, for hours, I walked the streets of London; through neighborhoods and squares, I wandered with no plan and no map. I wanted to see the houses and streets where people's lives happened. So I walked and I got lost and I learned to have faith.

I trace my wandering footsteps to the streets of the largest market in Cairo: *Khan el Khalili*. The narrow alleys of this market are filled with myriad shops and kiosks selling everything from belly dancing outfits, backgammon sets, and Pharaonic gods to pots and pans, copper trays, and rugs. If you don't buy something when you see it, you will lose yourself as you try to retrace your steps through the winding paths back to the same shop. One night, as we searched for a backgammon set from one shop to the next and then decided to return to the first one, we were led into a pattern of spirals until, I hate to admit it, my husband returned us to the original shop. Past midnight, we found ourselves with our friends, Maggie and Ayman, bargaining for a mother-of-pearl inlaid backgammon set. After an hour of back and forth offers that attracted at least six people, each choosing their side, we left with our successful purchase. Our shopping expedition concluded with eating *fetir* at a place that Maggie and Ayman knew, tucked alongside the shops. Our daughters watched the cook stretching and twirling the dough into a thin layer threatening to tear. It remained intact and arrived at our table, one filled with sharp cheese and another sweetened with powdered sugar.

I've learned to get lost with ease, certain that I will arrive at an acceptable destination. Unfortunately, Celine has not inherited my ability to keep calm when she loses her way. Now that she has been awarded her license, whenever she goes out, my husband and I remain in a state of suspended panic until she returns. If the phone rings and it's her, we have to decipher, through her shrill cries and sputtered words, where she is and how to guide her back to a familiar place. My attempt to tell her that all she has to do is follow the road and trust her instincts does little to help.

***

I disagree with my husband's assessment of my sense of direction. There are certain places I can always find. I present the following evidence:

- Early morning in Egypt, Yasmine and I walk to Tseppas pastry shop. I know that we can step out of our apartment building, take a right and then a left by the car always parked on the sidewalk and another right after the small kiosk selling fresh pita bread and then walk past the fruit seller where we buy the small yellow guavas to arrive at the same time as the truck delivering the pastries. The young man who works at the shop hands each of us a piece of konafa with cream, fresh and warm from the oven, his silent gift offered like a communion.
- We return to Egypt every eight years or so. Each time, we are invited to my relative's homes and I have to find my way. Addresses are elusive in Egypt—when I address Christmas cards to my family, I have to write things like "9 Mahmoud Ismail Street / From Abd el Aziz Ali Street or 43 El Gazair Street, Building 7/4." Street signs are rare, and as we walk through a neighborhood, I have only the imbedded memory of my past visits to guide me. Hunting by instinct, I walk, my husband insisting that the house we're looking for is one way or the other, but here I demand that he follows me. Inevitably, I look up to find my Uncle Fouad's apartment building, tucked down an alley barely visible from the main street. My husband flounders, having been certain that the building could not have been here, but his logic is no match for the streets of Cairo.

***

There are no highlighted lines on the map for me to follow. I was born to a life in the crowded city of Cairo, to repeat the pattern of each generation's hope—a doctor husband, an apartment in Zamalek, shopping trips to the City Stars Mall in Heliopolis, children at the British International School. I should have witnessed Sadat's assassination, Mubarak's demise, Morsi's election, El Sisi's victory. Instead I find myself living in a Tudor home, writing and teaching at a small college in southwestern Virginia, tying threads across the passage of ocean to my African American husband, to my children born of this unexpected journey, all of us unwinding the path from one continent to another.

RESOURCES

Further Reading

The Language of Baklava: A Memoir by Diana Abu-Jaber (Anchor Books, 2005)

At Home: Essays on Place and Displacement edited by Marjorie Agosín (Solis Press of the United Kingdom, 2015)

Cairo Workbook by TJ Anderson III (Willow Books, 2014)

Talking through the Door: An Anthology of Contemporary Middle Eastern American Writing, edited by Susan Atefat-Peckham (Syracuse University Press, 2014)

Tasting the Sky by Ibtisam Barakat (Square Fish, 2016)

Louder Than Hearts by Zeina Hashem Beck (Bauhan, 2017)

Stage Warriors: Women on the Front Lines of Dangerous Drama by Sarah Imes Borden (Cune Press, 2015)

Language for a New Century: Contemporary Poetry from The Middle East, Asia and Beyond, edited by Tina Chang, Nathalie Handal and Ravi Shankar (Norton, 2008)

Inclined to Speak edited by Hayan Charara (University of Arkansas Press 2008)

The Latin Deli: Telling the Lives of Barrio Women by Judith Oritz Cofer (Norton, 1995)

The Inheritance of Exile by Susan Muaddi Darraj (University of Notre Dame Press, 2007)

Funny in Farsi: A Memoir of Growing Up Iranian in America by Firoozeh Dumas (Random House, 2004)

Flying Carpets by Hedy Habra (Interlink, 2013)

The Girl in the Tangerine Scarf by Mohja Kahf (Hatchett, 2006)

Hope and Other Dangerous Pursuits by Laila Lalami (Harvest Books, 2006)

Geographies of Light by Lisa Suhair Majaj (Del Sol Press, 2009)

Arab America: Gender, Cultural Politics, and Activism by Nadine Naber (NYU Press, 2012)

Curse of the Achille Lauro: A Tribute to Lost Souls by Reem al-Nimer (Cune Press, 2014)

Never in a Hurry: Essays on People and Places by Naomi Shihab Nye (University of South Carolina Press, 1996)

Remember Me to Lebanon by Evelyn Shakir (Syracuse University Press, 2007)

Tahrir Suite by Matthew Shenoda (Triquarterly, 2014)

Homeland: Women's Journeys Across Race, Place and Time, edited by Patricia Justine Tumang and Henesha De Rivera (Seal Press, 2006)

Acknowledgements

My most sincere thanks to Lisa Suhair Majaj who believed in this book and found a home for it. Her guidance and editorial advice helped to make this a stronger work. My gratitude also goes to Scott C. Davis at Cune Press who accepted the book and brought it to life.

My appreciation goes to Hollins University and especially the audience at the Writers Harvest Readings who served as great listeners for several of these essays. Special thanks goes to Cara Modisett and the Liminal Art Gallery at Community High School in Roanoke, VA for the exhibits and the related prompts that motivated my writing.

I continue to be indebted to many who have supported my work, including Marjorie Agosín, Judith Ortiz Cofer, and Khaled Mattawa. Additional thanks goes to Courtney Flerlage who read early versions of many of these essays and offered excellent suggestions. And special thanks to Helen Zughaib for her beautiful art work titled "Teta's Key" that appears on the cover. (For more on Helen Zughaib: www. hzughaib.com).

I am deeply grateful to my husband, TJ Anderson III, and my two daughters, Yasmine and Celine, who helped me to laugh and inspired many of these stories.

Credits

"Among Neighbors" was originally published in *The Kindness of Strangers*, edited by Charles Brockett and Heather Tosteson (Wising Up Press, Decatur, GA: 2016).

"The Artistry of Circumstance" was originally published in *Gravel* (2016).

"Aunt Helena" was originally published in Borderlands and Crossroads: Writing the *Motherland*, edited by Jane Satterfield and Laurie Kruk (Demeter Press, Ontario, Canada, 2016).

"The Camel Caper" was originally published in *The Clinch Mountain Review* (2011).

"Exchange 81" was originally published in *The Clinch Mountain Review* (2015).

"The History of My Accent" was originally published in *Let the Bucket Down* (2015).

"Mediterranean Waves" was originally published in *Mediterranean Poetry* (http://www.odyssey.pm/, March 24, 2012).

"Name: An Improvisation on Sound" was originally published in *The Evansville Review* (2016).

"Nostalgia for Home" was originally published as part of the essay, "In the Direction of Home" in *At Home: Essays on Place and Displacement*, edited by Marjorie Agosín (Solis Press of the United Kingdom, 2015).

"To Walk Cautiously in the World" was originally published in *The Roanoke Times* (May 15, 2011).

Index

Aswat: Voices from a Small Planet

Looking Both Ways is part of a new series from Cune Press that features authors writing from their own experience. Aswat (Arabic for "voices") provides a space for voices that are honest, questioning, contemplative, and courageous: voices that narrate lives, challenge boundaries, map new geographies, or remap old ones. We have a special focus on writers with a connection to the Middle East, Asia, and Africa.

Pauline Kaldas

was born in Egypt and immigrated with her parents to the United States at the age of eight in 1969. She is the author of several books, and her work has appeared in a variety of anthologies, including *Inclined to Speak, Talking through the Door, At Home: Essays on Place and Displacement,* and *Others Will Enter the Gates.* She was awarded a fellowship in fiction from the Virginia Commission for the Arts, the Silver Award for *Dinarzad's Children* from *ForeWord Magazine* Book of the Year Awards, and the RAWI Creative Prose Award. She is Associate Professor of English and Creative Writing at Hollins University in Roanoke, Virginia.

Other Books by Pauline Kaldas

The Time between Places (short stories), University of Arkansas Press, 2010
Letters from Cairo (travel memoir), Syracuse University Press, 2007
Egyptian Compass (poetry), WordTech Communications, 2006
Dinarzad's Children: An Anthology of Contemporary Arab American Fiction
    (co-edited with Khaled Mattawa), University of Arkansas Press, 2009

Made in the USA
Lexington, KY
03 April 2017